COOKING WITH FRAGILE HANDS

by

Beverly Bingham, O.T.R.
Dame Maître Rôtisseur

CREATIVE CUISINE, INC.

COOKING WITH FRAGILE HANDS
BY BEVERLY BINGHAM

Photography by Beverly Bingham and Andrea Michaelsen
Cover Photograph by Steve Culver
Cover Design by Paul Wingo

Produced by Wright & Ratzlaff Associates

Published by Creative Cuisine, Inc.
P.O. Box 518
Naples, Florida 33939

Library of Congress Card No. 84-73054

Quality Hardcover Edition
ISBN 0-9614122-0-8
Retail Price $18.50

Trade Deluxe Softback Edition
ISBN: 0-9614122-1-6
Retail Price $15.50

Printed in the United States of America

DEDICATED TO ANNA

COOKING WITH FRAGILE HANDS

Preface

All of us who like to cook, I am sure, prefer to work from fresh produce and do as much as we can from "scratch." However we are not always masters of our fate. Arthritis and M.S. hit anyone from an early age to old age. Arthritis in particular is bound to no definite age.

The recipes in this book, when possible, utilize food that has been partially "prepped" such as frozen diced onions or freeze dried minced onions. No, they are not the same as fresh but if that one short cut makes it possible for you to cook then it is worth it. Compromises have to be made when hands cannot do the tasks that we would like them to do. All of us who suffer from Arthritis or M.S. know that some days it is impossible to go that "extra mile" in using fresh produce. Do what your hands will allow you without having undue fatigue or stress on your joints and body.

I have not put the number of portions that a recipe will serve for this reason -people's appetites vary tremendously depending upon their size, age and life styles. As an example - a chicken breast - for some it is too much for others not enough. I think you will be able to tell by looking at the recipe if it is about right for the number you are serving whether it be family or guests.

I have attempted to cover, in this book, almost everything that would be kitchen related. Look at the Table of Contents to guide you to the chapter that would be of help. The pictures I hope will stimulate your thoughts as to what you think would work for you. You will find out as you work from this book that it is far more than a cookbook. It is a means to help you become independent in the kitchen. Go to it!

Acknowledgments

I would like to thank the hundreds of Occupational Therapists and their patients who filled out my questionnaires and wrote letters of encouragement. It was their input that helped me greatly in putting this book together.

There are many people who ate, tested and critiqued the recipes in this book, however Murph and Betty Doty did more than anyone else and I thank you both for your help.

There were people who loaned their kitchen to be photographed, Karin and Eric Hakanson and Andrea and George Michaelsen. Don and Trudy Mattson uncomplainingly ran all over southwest Florida coping with last minute photographic needs. Graphic Systems, Minneapolis, Minnesota, and Anders Himmelstrup in particular, painstakingly did all the right things to make the cover turn out so well. Jerry Mathiason Photography did most of the black and white prints.

Kitchens by Krengel, St. Paul, Minnesota, Kitchens Unique and St. Charles Kitchens, Edina, Minnesota. All were so helpful in the photographing of their kitchens.

R.J. Schipper of Jennings, Naples, Florida, opened his store for photography. I also appreciate all the help that Sir Speedy of Naples gave me. Several people helped behind the scenes in a major way: Gran Harlow, Dan Daudon and John McNeil.

I greatly thank Connie Palmer O.T.R. who gave so freely of her evenings to discuss the book, look at copy and pictures and generally help in any way possible.

Betty Wright and company of Rainbow Books guided me, did the typesetting, the layout and multitudinous other things to get the book ready for Linda Monds at R.R. Donnelly who has done such a superb printing job.

Contents

Appetizers

Appetizers

Salmon Spread

Ingredients

Step One

1 cup cooked or canned salmon

Step Two

3 hard cooked eggs
1/4 cup mayonnaise
1 teaspoon Tabasco
2 Tablespoons minced celery
1 teaspoon tomato paste
2 teaspoons lemon juice
salt and pepper

Shopping List

1 small can salmon or 1 cup cooked
   salmon
3 eggs
1/4 cup mayonnaise
1 teaspoon Tabasco
1 stalk celery
1 teaspoon tomato paste
2 teaspoons lemon juice
salt
pepper

Method

Remove all bones, skin and fat.

Put all ingredients of Step One and Two into bowl of food processor fitted with steel blade and blend. This also may be blended by hand. Spread on canapes.

Utensils

can opener
measuring spoon
measuring cup
food processor optional
mixing bowl if done by hand
fork
knife

15

Kipper Paté

Ingredients

Step One

3 cans kippers
1/4 # butter
2 oz. cream cheese softened
1 teaspoon anchovy paste
1/8 teaspoon ground cloves
1/8 teaspoon mace or nutmeg
1 pinch of white pepper

Serve chilled on crackers or rounds of toast.

Method

Drain kippers. Mix all ingredients of Step One together in a food processor. Chill.

Shopping List

3 cans kippers
1/4 # butter
2 oz. cream cheese
1 teaspoon anchovy paste
ground cloves
mace or nutmeg
white pepper

Utensils

mixing bowl
wooden spoon
measuring spoon
can opener
food processor

Deviled Ham Spread

Ingredients

Step One

2 (4 ½ oz.) cans deviled ham
8 oz. cream cheese softened
1 Tablespoon catsup
1/2 teaspoon dijon style mustard
1 teaspoon dried minced onion

Step Two

Slice stuffed green olives

Shopping List

2 (4 ½ oz.) canned deviled ham
8 oz. cream cheese
catsup
dry minced onion
green stuffed olives

Method

Mix together in 1 qt. bowl.
Spread deviled ham on crackers and
garnish with sliced stuffed olives.

Utensils

1 qt. bowl
wooden spoon
measuring spoon
can opener
knife

Langostino Paté

Rock shrimp or lobster
may be substituted

Ingredients

Step One

4 oz. butter

Step Two

4 oz. cream cheese
6 oz. langostinos

Step Three

1/8 teaspoon nutmeg

Method

Melt and clarify.

Combine in food processor thawed langostinos and cream cheese with on/off pulse until cream texture.

Add nutmeg to clarified butter in a bowl large enough to hold langostinos mixture. Combine butter and langostinos mixture well. Fill serving cup and refrigerate. Serve with crackers or melba toast.

Shopping List

4 oz. butter
4 oz. cream cheese
6 oz. langostino
1/8 teaspoon nutmeg

Utensils

saucepan
food processor
spatula
bowl
measuring spoon
knife
serving container

Notes

Curried Crab Mold

Ingredients

Method

Step One

16 oz. softened cream cheese
1/2 cup curried mayonnaise*

Whirl in processor until well blended. Put on serving plate in the shape of a slightly mounded pancake.

Step Two

14-16 oz. crabmeat

Either canned or frozen well drained and patted dry. Go through crab for broken shells and cartilege. Put crab-meat on top of cream cheese mixture.

Step Three

2 hard cooked eggs

Peel and grate by hand over the crabmeat.

Step Four

1/4 cup frozen chopped chives

Thaw and pat dry - then sprinkle on top of grated eggs. Garnish with parsley if desired. Keep chilled until ready to use. Serve with crackers.

*See Curried Mayonnaise

Shopping List

16 oz. cream cheese
1/2 cup curried mayonnaise
14-16 oz. crabmeat frozen or canned
2 eggs
1/4 cup frozen chopped chives

Utensils

food processor or
electric mixer
plastic spatula
grater
can opener
knife
blunt knife
paper towels
measuring cup

Notes

Curried Mayonnaise

Ingredients

Step One

1 pint of mayonnaise

Step Two

1 Tablespoon curry powder
(Crosse & Blackwell type)
1 Tablespoon corn oil

Shopping List

1 pint of mayonnaise
1 Tablespoon curry powder
(Crosse & Blackwell type)
1 Tablespoon corn oil

Method

Put in a bowl.

Heat oil in a small pan over low heat and add curry. Stir continually. After about 1-2 minutes add warm curry to mayonnaise and mix well with a whisk. Put in a jar with a tight fitting lid. Store in refrigerator.

Utensils

small pan
measuring spoon
measuring cup
whisk
spoon
bowl

Walnut Cheese Log

Ingredients

Step One

10 oz. butter softened
20 oz. crumbled blue cheese
20 oz. softened cream cheese
1/4 cup minced dry onions
1½ teaspoon dry mustard
1½ oz. brandy

Step Two

1 cup walnuts
green olives

Shopping List

10 oz. butter
20 oz. cream cheese
20 oz. crumbled blue cheese
1/4 cup minced dry onions
dry mustard
brandy
1 cup walnuts
3-4 green olives

Method

Mix with electric mixer. Firm up in refrigerator then shape into log. Put on serving plate and chill.

Finely chop in food processor. Sprinkle on log. Cut olives in quarters and garnish log.

Utensils

electric mixer
bowl
spatula
measuring cup
knife
serving plate
food processor

Chutney Cheese

Ingredients

Step One

2 oz. crumbled blue cheese
8 oz. cream cheese
1/3 cup Major Gray's chutney

Step Two

Step Three

Shopping List

2 oz. crumbled blue cheese
8 oz. cream cheese
1/3 cup Major Gray's chutney

Method

Puree in food processor.

Scoop mixture from food processor into a container that you can serve it in. Chill.

When almost set, smooth off top with wet knife and cover with plastic wrap.

Utensils

food processor
spatula
knife
container to serve cheese in

Sweet and Sour Meatballs

Ingredients

Step One

1 # ground beef
1/2 cup diced mushrooms
2 Tablespoons minced dry chives
1 Tablespoon minced dry onions
1/2 teaspoon salt, dash of pepper
1/2 teaspoon Beau Monde seasoning
1/2 teaspoon dry mustard
1 egg
1/4 cup bread crumbs
Dash of milk

Step Two

Sauce

2 cups grape jelly
2 cups barbecue sauce
3 oz. tomato paste

Method

Mix all of ingredients of Step One together with hands. Form into meatballs the size of a walnut.

Put on a shallow baking sheet. Bake at 350° for 15 minutes.

Simmer over low heat for 1 hour being careful not to scorch it.

This freezes very well in sauce. Be sure meatballs are completely covered. Serve with toothpicks.

Shopping List

1 # ground beef
1/4 # mushrooms
2 Tablespoons minced dry chives
1 Tablespoon minced dry onions
salt and pepper
Beau Monde seasoning
dry mustard
1 egg
1/4 cup bread crumbs
dash of milk
2 cups grape jelly
2 cups barbecue sauce
3 oz. tomato paste

Utensils

bowl large enough to mix
dry ingredients
2 qt. saucepan
measuring cup
measuring spoons
knife or food processor
shallow baking sheet

Notes

Herb Deviled Eggs

Ingredients

Step One

6 hard cooked eggs
3-4 teaspoons mayonnaise

Step Two

2 pinches tarragon
1/4 teaspoon dry mustard
salt and pepper

Shopping List

6 eggs
3-4 teaspoons mayonnaise
tarragon
dry mustard
salt and pepper

Method

Halve eggs, scoop out egg yolks and mash by hand or with electric mixer. Mix in mayonnaise — the amount depends upon size of egg.

Grind tarragon in the palms of hand. Add all of Step Two to Step One.

Fill egg whites with yolk mixture garnish with tiny piece of parsley.

Utensils

fork
electric mixer optional
bowl
measuring spoon
knife
saucepan to cook eggs

Spicy Deviled Eggs

Ingredients

Step One

6 hard cooked eggs

Step Two

1 teaspoon anchovy paste
3 Tablespoons sour cream
1 Tablespoon mayonnaise
6 capers finely minced
12 dashes Tabasco
2-3 drops lemon juice
pinch of tarragon

Shopping List

6 eggs
anchovy paste
3 Tablespoons sour cream
1 Tablespoon mayonnaise
6 capers
Tabasco
2-3 drops lemon juice
tarragon

Method

Electric mixer advised. Peel and halve the eggs. Scoop out yolk and put into mixing bowl. Lay egg whites on plate.

Mash egg yolks. Using an electric mixer combine all of Step Two into egg yolks. Fill whites with egg yolk mixture. Garnish with a sprig of parsley.

Utensils

saucepan to boil eggs — to cook
fork
electric mixer
mixing bowl
measuring bowl
measuring spoons
spoon
knife
plate

Rolled Appetizers

General Instructions

Use a soft bread such as Wonderbread. Remove crusts with a knife. Roll the slices of bread with a rolling pin. Each slice will make 3 appetizers.

Notes

Rolled Asparagus

Ingredients

Step One

8 oz. cream cheese softened
2 Tablespoons cream

Step Two

1 can high quality asparagus

Step Three

1/4 # melted butter

Shopping List

8 oz. cream cheese
2 Tablespoons cream
1 can high quality asparagus
1/4 # butter
soft bread

Method

Mix together and spread on slice of rolled soft bread.

Drain asparagus. Put spear on bottom end of slice and roll up. Put roll seam side down on baking sheet.

Baste roll with a pastry brush. Bake at 350 ° for 12 - 15 minutes until golden. Cut into thirds.

Utensils

can opener
fork
bowl large enough to hold cheese
saucepan to melt butter
rolling pin
knife
pastry brush
baking sheet
tooth pick to serve with

Rolled Spinach and Mushrooms

Ingredients

Step One

10 oz. frozen chopped spinach

Step Two

1/2 # mushrooms

Step Three

2 oz. butter
2 teaspoons minced dry onions
reserved spinach

Step Four

8 oz. cream cheese softened

Method

Step One

Thaw and squeeze moisture out by pressing gently through a strainer. Set aside.

Step Two

Clean and dice either by hand or with food processor.

Step Three

Melt butter in skillet - add diced mushrooms and minced dry onions. Sauté mushrooms until all liquid has been released and moisture has evaporated. Add spinach and cook until dry.

Step Four

Add cream cheese to spinach/mushroom mixture and mix well.

Step Five

Rolled soft bread	Spread on rolled bread. Roll up and place seam side down on baking sheet.
1/4 # melted butter	Baste with melted butter. Bake in 350° oven for 12 - 15 minutes. Cut into thirds.

Shopping List

10 oz. frozen chopped spinach
1/2 # mushrooms
soft bread
2 teaspoons dry minced onions
6 oz. butter
8 oz. cream cheese

Utensils

strainer
medium sized bowl
knife
rolling pin
spatula
fork
measuring spoon
spreading knife
skillet
basting brush
baking sheet

Notes

Onion - Mayonnaise Canapés

Ingredients

Step One

4 slices very thin white bread

Method

Remove crusts and cut into 4 squares or cut into 4 rounds without removing crusts.

Step Two

1 Tablespoon dried minced onions
1/2 cup mayonnaise

Mix together and spread on rounds.

Shopping List

4 slices thin white bread
1 Tablespoon dried minced onions
1/2 cup mayonnaise
16 rounds

Utensils

knife or circle cutter
measuring spoon
measuring cup
small bowl
cookie sheet

Ham and Cheese Morsels

Ingredients

Method

Step One

6 slices of bread
dijon style mustard

Spread one side of bread with
mustard.

Step Two

3 slices ham or enough to cover slices
    of bread
3 slices Swiss cheese

Lay ham on 3 pieces of bread. Place
cheese on ham. Place remaining bread
on top of ham and cheese. Mustard
side on cheese.

Step Three

1 egg lightly beaten
1 cup cream
salt
pepper

Mix egg and cream together in a bowl
or dish wide enough to lay bread
down.

Step Four

Dip sandwich into batter covering
both sides. Bake on cookie sheet at
350° until under side is golden - turn
over continue baking until other side
is golden. Cool slightly. Cut off crusts
and cut into triangles. Refrigerate &
reheat when ready to serve at 350° for
10 minutes.

Shopping List

6 slices bread
dijon style mustard
3 slices of ham
3 slices Swiss cheese
1 egg
1 cup light cream

Utensils

spreader
knife
cookie sheet
wide mouth bowl or plate
metal spatula

Notes

Cheese-Pecan Crisps

Ingredients

Step One

1/2 # grated sharp cheddar

Step Two

4 oz. butter

Step Three

1¼ cup flour
1 Tablespoon Worcestershire sauce
1/2 teaspoon salt
dash cayenne
1 Tablespoon Amaretto
1 cup finely chopped pecans

Step Four

Method

Either purchase grated cheese or grate with food processor.

Cream butter and cheese together either by hand or with food processor.

Mix Step Three into Step Two.

Refrigerate then roll into a roll about 1½" in diameter, wrap in wax paper and put in freezer. When hardened slice into thin rounds. Bake on ungreased cookie sheet at 350° for 8-10 minutes.

Shopping List

1/2 # grated sharp cheddar cheese
4 oz. butter
1¼ cup flour
Worcestershire sauce
salt
1 Tablespoon Amaretto
1 cup finely chopped pecans
cayenne

Utensils

food processor
measuring spoon
measuring cup
scissors
wax paper
cookie sheet
spatula

Notes

Cheese-Walnut Wafers

Ingredients

Step One

1/2 # sharp cheddar

Step Two

4 oz. butter

Step Three

1 Tablespoon Worcestershire sauce
1¼ cup flour
1/2 teaspoon salt
pinch of red pepper
6 drops Tabasco sauce
1 cup finely ground walnuts that have
  been through food processor

Step Four

Method

Grate with food processor.

Cream butter and cheese together by mixer or with food processor.

Add all ingredients to mixer or food processor.

Refrigerate until able to form into rolls the size of a half dollar. Put rolls in freezer to firm up. Slice into thin wafers. Bake on ungreased cookie sheet for 10 minutes at 350° or until lightly golden around the edges. Store in tin.

Shopping List

1/2 # cheddar cheese
4 oz. butter
1 Tablespoon Worcestershire sauce
1¼ cups flour
1/2 teaspoon salt
red pepper
Tabasco sauce
8 oz. walnut pieces

Utensils

food processor
knife
aluminum foil or wax paper
hand grater optional
measuring cup
measuring spoon
cookie sheet
spatula rubber & metal

Notes

General Preparation for Mushroom Caps

1. Clean mushroom caps with a brush
2. Remove stems and set aside
3. Butter baking sheet
4. Place caps hollow-side down on baking sheet
5. Bake in 350° oven for 10 minutes
6. Cool
7. Stuff with prepared stuffing

Stuffed Mushrooms: stuffed mushrooms are very adaptable creatures to serve. The stuffing freezes very well. The food processor makes dicing the mushrooms a snap. I have found rather than doing many small batches of stuffed mushrooms, which in turn means washing bowls and pans many times, that it is easier to do one larger batch. This is an ideal place for a spouse, friend or companion to lend a hand. Try making a large batch of stuffing or a variety of stuffings. Then package the stuffing in small containers that would hold the amount needed for one night's entertaining. For instance if you normally have six people for dinner and you would like your guests to have three per person then package enough stuffing to fill 18 medium sized mushroom caps. Freeze these containers of stuffing and then thaw as needed. However do remember to mark the containers. It can be quite annoying to think you are serving mushrooms stuffed with crabmeat and find out as it is cooking that you will be serving Mushrooms Provençal. The stuffing may be frozen for up to two months.

Mushroom Caps Stuffed with Sausage

Ingredients

Step One

36 medium - large mushrooms

Step Two

1/4 cup butter (2 oz.)
2 cloves garlic minced
  or 1/4 teaspoon garlic powder

Step Three

1 teaspoon of herbs of provence*
8 oz. bulk sausage

Step Four

1/4 cup bread crumbs
1/4 cup grated parmesan cheese
2 Tablespoons minced parsley

Method

Step One

Prepare mushroom caps in the usual manner - removing stems and chopping them by hand or with a food processor.

Step Two

Melt butter, sauté stems in melted butter with garlic until stems have released their moisture and moisture has evaporated. Set aside.

Step Three

In same pan as above sauté until brown - separating clumps of meat.

Step Four

Mix together then stir into Step Three.

Mix in cooked mushroom stems.

Step Five

parmesan cheese

Fill caps in usual manner. Sprinkle parmesan cheese on top. Bake 10 minutes at 350° or until heated through.

*Provence herbs equal parts thyme, basil, summer savory and fennel

Hint: If you like to use provençal herbs in your cooking, make a sizeable batch and mix well. Store in a jar with a tightly fitting lid in the refrigerator.

Shopping List

36 medium - large mushrooms
4 oz. butter
2 cloves garlic
   or 1/4 teaspoon garlic powder
thyme
basil
summer savory
fennel
8 oz. bulk sausage
1/4 cup bread crumbs
3-4 oz. grated parmesan cheese
2 Tablespoons minced dry parsley

Utensils

food processor
skillet
measuring spoons
measuring cups
cookie sheet with sides
pastry brush
small bowl

Mushroom Caps Stuffed with Crabmeat

Ingredients

Step One

5-6 oz. mushroom stems or whole
  mushrooms

Step Two

3 Tablespoons butter
1 Tablespoon flour
1/2 cup milk or half & half
2 oz. cream cheese

Step Three

2½ Tablespoons butter
1/2 cup frozen chopped chives
diced mushroom stems

Step Four

5 oz. crab
1½ Tablespoons brandy
dash of Tabasco

Method

Remove stems from caps. Dice them medium fine either with a food processor or by hand. There should be about 1¼ cups.

Melt butter in a skillet. Add flour and whisk about 1-2 minutes. Gradually add liquid and blend. No lumps please. Blend in the cream cheese. Set aside in a bowl. Rinse out skillet.

Melt butter, add chives and mushroom stems. Cook until liquid has been released and moisture evaporated.

Go over crabmeat removing any hard particles. Add crabmeat to mushrooms. Stir in brandy. Combine with sauce.

Step Five

1/4 cup parmesan cheese

Stuffing may be made ahead and frozen.

Stuff in usual manner.

Sprinkle on top of mushrooms. Bake in 350° oven 10 minutes or until heated through.

Shopping List

1 # mushrooms
5½ Tablespoons butter
1 Tablespoon flour
1/2 cup milk or half & half
2 oz. cream cheese
1/2 cup frozen chopped chives
5 oz. crabmeat
1½ Tablespoons brandy
dash of Tabasco
1/4 cup grated parmesan

Utensils

baking sheet
pastry brush
food processor
knife
measuring cup
measuring spoon
skillet
bowl
spoon

Notes

Mushrooms with Escargot

Ingredients

Step One

1½ dz. mushroom caps

Step Two

1/2 cup butter (4 oz.)

Step Three

4 cloves garlic or equivalent amount
   refrigerated in jar
1 teaspoon minced dried parsley
1 teaspoon minced dry onions
2 teaspoon dried chopped chives

Step Four

18 snails

Method

Prepare in usual manner.

Melt.

Add all of Step Three to Step Two.

Wash well and put one snail in each
mushroom cap. Pour seasoned butter
over it. Bake at 350° for 8-10 minutes.

Shopping List

1½ dz. mushrooms
1½ dz. snails
4 oz. butter
4 cloves of garlic or equivalent
1 teaspoon minced dried parsley
1 teaspoon minced dry onions
2 teaspoon dried chopped chives

Utensils

knife
can opener
cookie sheet
spoon
saucepan
measuring spoon

Notes

Mushrooms Provençal

Ingredients

Step One

Prepare mushroom caps in usual manner.

Step Two

2 # mushrooms
4 oz. butter

Step Three

1 cup fine bread crumbs
1/2 cup grated parmesan
hearty pinch of thyme
1/8 teaspoon garlic powder

Step Four

2 Tablespoons cream cheese
splash of milk

Method

Dice by processor. Melt butter and sauté mushrooms until all liquid has been released and moisture has evaporated. Put in medium sized bowl.

Add to mushrooms and mix well.

Put cream cheese and milk into skillet in which mushrooms have been cooked. Melt cream cheese add to diced mushrooms.

Step Five

Either freeze filling in desired amounts or fill caps in usual manner.

Shopping List

2 # mushrooms
4 oz. butter
1 cup fine bread crumbs
1/2 cup grated parmesan
thyme
garlic powder
2 Tablespoons cream cheese
splash of milk

Utensils

food processor
knife
measuring spoon
measuring cup
medium sized bowl
skillet large enough
  to hold mushrooms
containers to freeze stuffing
  if desired

Notes

Soups

Soups

Curried Tomato Bisque

Ingredients

Step One

1 Tablespoon butter
6 oz. frozen chopped onions
1/8 scant teaspoon garlic powder
1¼ teaspoons curry powder

Step Two

1 can (28 oz.) can peeled
   Italian plum tomatoes
1/4 of a bay leaf
1/4 teaspoon thyme
1/4 cup raw long grain rice
10 oz. canned chicken broth
3 drops Tabasco

Step Three

Method

Food processor or electric blender.

Melt butter in a 2 qt. saucepan. Add garlic and onion. Cook onion until wilted. Sprinkle curry powder over onions. Cook approximately 3 minutes longer stirring continually.

Add all of Step Two to Step One. Partially cover pan and simmer 45 minutes.

Put small batches of soup either through processor or blender.

Step Four

1 cup cold milk
1/2 cup cream

When cool stir milk and cream into soup. Serve either hot or cold with a dollop of sour cream.

Shopping List

1 Tablespoon butter
1 can chicken broth
1 can (28 oz.) peeled
   Italian plum tomatoes
6 oz. frozen chopped onions
1/4 cup long grain rice
curry powder
garlic powder
bay leaf
thyme
Tabasco
sour cream (optional)
1/2 cup cream
1 cup cold milk

Utensils

knife
can opener
measuring spoons
measuring cups
2 qt. saucepan with lid
food processor
   or
electric blender
large spoon or whisk
bowl to put finished purée in - to mix
   with milk

Notes

Cold Vegetable Soup

Ingredients

Step One

2 Tablespoons butter

Step Two

2 stalks celery
10 oz. frozen chopped spinach
1 zucchini

Step Three

1 can shrimp soup
1 can tomato bisque
1½ cups half & half
1 packet dried onion soup mix
1 oz. sherry

Method

Melt.

Cut celery and zucchini into one inch pieces. Thaw and drain spinach. Sauté 5 minutes over moderate heat. Do not brown. Put through blender.

While vegetables are sautéing mix Step Three ingredients together in a saucepan.

Step Four

sour cream
champagne vinegar

In the above saucepan combine blended vegetables and soup mixture. Cook briefly then chill well before serving.

Serve with a dollop of sour cream. Pass the champagne vinegar — a sprinkle in each bowl cuts the sweetness for those that prefer a soup with a crisper flavor.

Shopping List

1 oz. butter
2 stalks celery
10 oz. chopped spinach
1 zucchini
1 can shrimp soup
1 can tomato bisque
1½ cups half & half
1 packet dried onion soup mix
1 oz. sherry
sour cream
champagne vinegar

Utensils

frying pan large enough
   to hold the vegetables
saucepan large enough
   for vegetables and soup
measuring spoons
measuring cups
knife
cutting board
blender or food processor

Notes

Curried Zucchini Soup

Ingredients

Step One

3/4 cup frozen chopped onions

Step Two

4 Tablespoons butter

Step Three

2 # zucchini
6 cups simmering chicken stock or
   broth
1/4 cup uncooked long grain rice
1 teaspoon curry

Step Four

Method

Thaw and pat dry onions on paper toweling.

Cook onions slowly in butter until translucent.

Cut zucchini into 2 inch segments. Add zucchini, rice and onions to stock. Simmer for 30 minutes. Add curry last five minutes. Cool.

When cool enough to handle put through food processor or blender and chill.

Step Five

2/3 cup heavy cream

Add to chilled soup. May be served hot or cold.

Shopping List

3/4 cup frozen chopped onions
2 # zucchini
6 cups chicken broth
1/4 cup uncooked long grain rice
1 teaspoon curry powder
2/3 cup heavy cream
4 Tablespoons butter

Utensils

small skillet or saucepan
knife
can opener
measuring cup
measuring spoon
4-5 qt. sauce pan

Notes

Cream of Sorrel Soup

Ingredients

Step One

1/3 cup chopped frozen onions

Step Two

3 Tablespoons butter

Step Three

4 cups sorrel
  reserve a few small
  leaves for garnish

Step Four

5½ cups simmering chicken broth
1/4 cup uncooked long grain rice

Step Five

1/2 cup cream
salt/pepper

Method

Thaw and pat dry on paper toweling.

Cook onions slowly until translucent.

Remove woody stems and heavy veins. Cut coarsely by hand or with food processor. Add to onions and cook 5 minutes.

Add sorrel and onions to rice and broth. Cook 15 minutes. Cool then put through food processor or blender. Chill.

Add to above and season to taste

Shopping List

1/3 cup frozen chopped onions
3 Tablespoons butter
3-4 bunches of sorrel
5½ cups of chicken broth or 3 cans
1/4 cup long grain rice
salt/pepper
1/2 cup cream

Utensils

measuring cup
knife
scissors
paper towels
small skillet
4-6 qt. saucepan
spoon
food processor or blender
large bowl to store soup in
can opener

Notes

Cream of Broccoli Soup

Ingredients

Step One

3/4 cup frozen diced onions
4 Tablespoons butter

Step Two

2 # frozen cut up broccoli
6 cups simmering chicken broth
1/4 cup uncooked long grain rice

Step Three

Step Four

2/3 cup half & half or milk

Method

Sauté in butter until onions are trans-lucent.

Add broccoli, onions and rice to chicken broth. Simmer for 25 minutes.

Put soup through a food processor or blender in small batches. Pour into large bowl large enough to hold all of soup.

Add cream to soup and mix well. May be served either hot or cold.

Shopping List

3/4 cup frozen diced onions
4 Tablespoons butter
2 # cut up broccoli
6 cups chicken broth
1/4 cup uncooked long grain rice
2/3 cup half & half

Utensils

small skillet
knife
measuring cup
4 qt. saucepan
processor or blender
bowl large enough to
 hold finished soup

Notes

Cream of Asparagus Soup

Ingredients

Step One

3/4 cup frozen diced onions
1/4 cup frozen diced chives
4 Tablespoons butter

Step Two

2 # asparagus

Step Three

6 cups chicken broth
1/4 cup uncooked long grain rice

Step Four

Method

Sauté in butter until translucent. Put into a 4 qt. saucepan or larger.

Cut off tough ends. Wash and clean well. Cut into 2 inch segments add to onions.

Add broth and rice to Step Two. Simmer for 25 minutes.

When cool enough to handle, put through processor or blender in small batches.

Step Five

2/3 cup half & half or milk

Add to above. May be served hot or cold. Season to taste.

Shopping List

3/4 cup frozen diced onions
1/4 cup frozen diced chives
4 Tablespoons butter
2 # asparagus
6 cups chicken broth
1/4 cup uncooked long grain rice
2/3 cup half and half or milk

Utensils

small skillet
spoon
knife
measuring cup
4 qt. saucepan
food processor or blender
bowl to hold finished soup

Notes

Cream of Cauliflower Soup

Ingredients

Step One

1/2 cup frozen chopped onions

Step Two

4 Tablespoons butter

Step Three

2 # frozen cauliflower buds
1/3 cup diced carrots
1 cup sliced celery
2 qts. simmering chicken stock
  or broth
1/4 cup uncooked long grain rice
1/2 teaspoon peppercorns
1/2 teaspoon dried tarragon
1/2 bay leaf

Step Four

Method

Thaw onions and pat dry on paper toweling.

Sauté onions in butter and reserve.

Dice carrots in food processor. Slice celery in food processor. Put vegetables in chicken broth with onions and simmer 30 minutes.

Remove peppercorns. Put all ingredients through a food processor or blender. Chill.

Step Five

2 cups milk
1 cup heavy cream
salt and pepper to taste

Add to chilled mixture. Serve hot or cold.

Shopping List

1/2 cup frozen chopped onions
4 Tablespoons butter
2 # frozen cauliflower buds
1 carrot
3-4 stalks celery
2 qt. chicken broth
rice
peppercorns
tarragon
bay leaf
2 cups milk
1 cup heavy cream
salt/pepper

Utensils

saucepan or skillet
knife
scissors
measuring cup
large pot
measuring spoon
blender or food processor
spoon (large)
paper toweling
can opener
bowl large enough to store soup

Notes

Pumpkin Soup

Ingredients

Step One

1 Tablespoon butter
1 cup frozen chopped onions
2 Tablespoons frozen chopped chives

Step Two

1 can (16 oz.) pumpkin puree
2½ cups chicken broth
1/2 teaspoon Beau Monde

Step Three

Step Four

1 cup half & half
1¼ cups sour cream
salt and pepper

Method

Electric blender or processor

Melt butter in 3 qt. saucepan. Saute onions and chives over low heat until onions are wilted.

Mix Step Two into Step One and simmer over low heat for 20 minutes. Cool then proceed with Step Three.

Put the above through a blender or processor in small batches.

Stir into cooled pumpkin mixture. Chill. Salt and pepper to taste.

1. May be served either hot or cold.
2. Garnish with a dollop of sour cream and a piece of popcorn if desired.

Shopping List

1 can (16 oz.) pumpkin puree
2½ cups chicken broth
1 cup frozen chopped onions
2 Tablespoons frozen chopped chives
1 Tablespoon butter
1 cup half & half
1¼ cup sour cream
1/2 teaspoon Beau Monde
salt and pepper

Utensils

3 qt. saucepan
whisk
measuring spoons
measuring cups
electric blender or processor
can opener
spoon or spatula

Notes

Chicken Soup Florentine

Ingredients

Step One

46 oz. chicken broth
2 Tablespoons dried minced onion
2 teaspoons seasoned salt
2 teaspoons celery seed
scant 1/2 teaspoon seasoned pepper

Step Two

1 can (16 oz.) Italian tomatoes

Step Three

1 10 oz. pkg. frozen chopped spinach

Optional: 2 oz. sherry

May be frozen

Method

Put all of Step One into kettle.

Drain and roughly cut or pull apart with fingers. Add to Step One and simmer 20 minutes.

Thaw and drain. Cook in skillet until dry. Add to broth and simmer an additional 5 minutes. Add sherry last 5 minutes.

Shopping List

46 oz. chicken broth
dried onion
seasoned salt and pepper
celery seed
16 oz. Italian tomatoes
10 oz. pkg. frozen chopped spinach
sherry optional

Utensils

measuring cup
measuring spoon
skillet
saucepan
wooden spoon
can opener
knife

Notes

Gazpacho Blanco

Ingredients

Step One

2 cucumbers
1/4 cup frozen diced onions
1 Tablespoon frozen diced chives
1 green pepper
3/4 cup chicken broth

Step Two

1/4 cup mayonnaise
1/4 cup sour cream
3 Tablespoons white wine vinegar
1 teaspoon salt
1 teaspoon Beau Monde seasoning
1/2 teaspoon pepper
3 Tablespoons dried dill weed

Step Three

3/4 cup chicken broth
sugar

Method

Food processor

Peel cucumber and cut into equal chunks. Remove seeds from pepper and cut into equal chunks. Puree all of Step One. Pour into bowl.

Mix all of Step Two together in bowl and then mix into Step One.

Mix broth into soup. Sugar may be needed if cucumbers are bitter. Chill.

Shopping List

2 cucumbers
1/4 cup frozen diced onions
1 Tablespoon frozen diced chives
1 green pepper
1 can chicken broth
1/4 cup mayonnaise
1/4 cup sour cream
3 Tablespoons white wine vinegar
1 teaspoon salt
1 teaspoon Beau Monde seasoning
1/2 teaspoon pepper
3 Tablespoons dried dill weed

Utensils

peeler
food processor or blender
knife
measuring cup
measuring spoon
large bowl

Notes

Gazpacho Soup

Ingredients

Step One

1 onion
1 pepper
1 cucumber

Step Two

2 cups tomato sauce

Step Three

2 cups tomato juice
1/4 cup olive oil
1½ teaspoon vinegar
1/4 teaspoon garlic powder
  or 2 cloves garlic
1 teaspoon salt
1/4 teaspoon cumin

Method

Skin and roughly cut onion. Seed and roughly cut pepper. Peel and roughly cut cucumber.

Using a food processor with a steel blade, put some of sauce in processor bowl. Add pepper, onion and cucumber. Puree mixture using pulsing on/off method. Pour into large bowl.

Add all of Step Three to Step Two and mix well. Store in jar with tight fitting lid. Should be made a day ahead. Keeps for many days in refrigerator.

Shopping List

16 oz. tomato sauce
16 oz. tomato juice
1 onion
1 pepper
1 cucumber
1/4 cup olive oil
1½ oz. vinegar
1/4 teaspoon garlic powder
   or
2 cloves garlic
salt
cumin

Utensils

food processor
can opener
knife
vegetable peeler
measuring cup
measuring spoons
2 qt. mixing bowl
garlic press optional

Notes

Beef Broth with Seasonings

Ingredients

Method

Step One

1 quart beef broth
1 can (16 oz.) Italian plum tomatoes
  well drained

Open cans and put into kettle.

Step Two

1 Tablespoon dried minced onions
1½ teaspoon seasoned salt
1/4 teaspoon seasoned pepper

Add to beef broth and tomatoes.
Simmer 30 minutes.

Hint: Some canned beef broth is quite
salty - do NOT add salt until the end
after you have tasted it.

May be frozen in individual servings.

Shopping List

1 qt. beef broth
1 can (16 oz.) Italian tomatoes
dried onion
seasoned salt and pepper

Utensils

saucepan
can opener
measuring spoons
large spoon

Notes

Main Dishes

Main Dishes

Chicken Breasts

The chicken recipes in this book use boned chicken breasts as eating the chicken with a fork and knife puts added stress on the joints. Many recipes call for the chicken breasts to be cut in finger length strips. The advantage of this is one, the chicken goes further and two, usually you do not need to use a knife as it should be fork tender. If you prefer to use a boneless breast without cutting it up that is fine. The recipes are equally adaptable either way.

Chicken breasts are often sold boneless or you can have the butcher bone it for you. If you are unable to slice them in finger length strips have the butcher, spouse or friend do it for you. Three boned chicken breasts cut into strips will serve four people. The strips of chicken breasts that you will use at a later date can be stored in single or double portions in a small plastic container with chicken broth. When chicken is called for in a recipe simply thaw the amount needed. The chicken broth is then used in the sauce.

Chicken Mediterranean

Ingredients

Method

Step One

4 boneless chicken breasts
  skin removed
small amount of oil

Brown chicken in oil. Transfer to large saucepan or skillet that will hold chicken and sauce.

Step Two

3/4 cup frozen diced onions
1 Tablespoon butter

Thaw, drain and pat dry onions. Sauté in same skillet that chicken was browned. Add to chicken.

Step Three

10 oz. sweet vermouth
2/3 cup canned Italian tomatoes
3/4 teaspoon basil
1/3 teaspoon thyme
1/8 teaspoon garlic powder

Drain tomatoes and pull apart. Add ingredients of Step Three to Step Two then pour into saucepan with chicken. Simmer 25-30 minutes.

Optional

1/2 # sliced mushrooms
2 Tablespoons butter

Sauté in skillet in which onions were cooked. Add to chicken when ready to serve.

May be made ahead and reheated. Not really enough sauce to freeze well. Tends to dry out. May substitute canned sliced mushrooms.

Shopping List

4 boneless chicken breasts
small amount of oil
3/4 cup frozen diced onions
3 Tablespoons butter
10 oz. sweet vermouth
1 small can Italian tomatoes
1/2 # mushrooms
basil
thyme
garlic powder

Utensils

skillet that will hold chicken
large saucepan or skillet
tongs
knife to cut butter
measuring spoons
measuring cup
wooden spoon
can opener
knife to slice mushrooms

Notes

Chicken and Artichoke Casserole

Ingredients

Step One

4 boneless chicken breasts
4 Tablespoons butter

Step Two

4 Tablespoons flour
10 oz. chicken broth
   room temperature

Step Three

4 oz. mozzarella cheese
   shredded
3 oz. Swiss cheese
   shredded
1 teaspoon Beau Monde seasoning
1/8 teaspoon garlic powder
1/3 cup sherry or madeira

Method

Skin and cut chicken into finger length strips. Melt butter in skillet. Sauté chicken until light golden. Remove chicken to casserole.

Add to butter in skillet and cook for 1-2 minutes. Add broth to roux stirring continually with whisk to remove any lumps.

Add all ingredients of Step Three to Step Two. Keep warm on very low heat.

Step Four

1/2 # mushrooms sliced
2 Tablespoons butter

Melt butter in frying pan. Add sliced mushrooms. Cook until mushrooms have released their juices and all moisture has evaporated.

Step Five

Add mushrooms to sauce. Pour over chicken in casserole.

Step Six

1 large can artichoke hearts NOT marinated

Drain and cut artichokes in half. Stir into chicken.

Step Seven

2 Tablespoons grated parmesan cheese

Sprinkle over top of casserole. Bake in 350° oven uncovered for 30 minutes.

Can be made ahead and reheated.

Shopping List

4 boned chicken breasts
6 Tablespoons butter
4 Tablespoons flour
10 oz. chicken broth
4 oz. mozzarella cheese shredded
3 oz. Swiss cheese shredded
1 teaspoon Beau Monde seasoning
1/8 teaspoon garlic powder
1/3 cup sherry or madeira
1/2 # mushrooms
1 can (14 oz.) artichoke hearts NOT
  marinated

Utensils

knife
skillet large enough to hold chicken
casserole
whisk
measuring cup
measuring spoons
spoon
can opener

Spinach Casserole with Chicken

Ingredients

Step One

2 frozen pkg. chopped spinach
1/2 cup sliced mushrooms
2 Tablespoons butter

Step Two

1½ pint sour cream
1 pkg. onion soup mix

Step Three

2 whole chicken breasts cooked
  and diced

Step Four

4 oz. grated cheddar cheese
3/4 cup herbed croutons which have
  been made into crumbs

Method

Mix together and add to Step One.

Grease casserole. Put 1/2 of spinach mixture in casserole. Then put chicken on top of spinach. Top the chicken with the remainder of the spinach.

Sprinkle chicken/spinach with cheese and crumbs. Bake at 350° for 30 minutes.

Shopping List

2 frozen pkg. chopped spinach
1/2 # mushrooms
2 Tablespoons butter
1½ pints sour cream
1 pkg. onion soup mix
2 whole chicken breasts cooked
  and diced
4 oz. grated cheddar
3/4 cup herbed croutons

Utensils

scissors
skillet
food processor or
  knife
ovenproof casserole
measuring cup

Notes

Broccoli-Chicken Casserole

Ingredients

Step One

2 pkg. frozen broccoli

Step Two

6 boneless chicken breasts
6 thin slices Canadian bacon
3 Tablespoons melted butter

Step Three

3 eggs
1 cup chopped celery
2 Tablespoons minced dry onions
1 Tablespoon lemon juice
1 teaspoon salt
1/8 teaspoon pepper
1/2 teaspoon basil

Step Four

16 oz. can Italian tomatoes
1/4 cup sweet vermouth
1/2 cup chicken broth

Method

Thaw and put aside broccoli in 6 equal parts.

Wrap first the Canadian bacon and then the chicken around the broccoli. Put them in a casserole in which the melted butter has been spread around.

Beat the eggs and add the other ingredients of Step Three to a mixing bowl large enough to hold the tomatoes also.

Drain and roughly cut tomatoes. Mix Step Four into Step Three.

84

Step Five

Pour Step Three over the broccoli and chicken.

Step Six

1 cup bread crumbs
1/2 cup slivered almonds
parmesan cheese optional

Sprinkle on top of the casserole. Sprinkle the parmesan if desired. Bake in 350° oven 35 minutes or until chicken is done. If more liquid is needed add a little water.

Shopping List

2 pkg. frozen broccoli
6 boneless chicken breasts
6 thin slices Canadian bacon
3 eggs
2-3 ribs of celery
minced dry onions
1/2 lemon
salt
pepper
basil
1 can (16 oz.) Italian tomatoes
1/4 cup sweet vermouth
1/2 cup chicken broth
1 cup bread crumbs
4 oz. slivered almonds
2 Tablespoons butter

Utensils

scissors
ovenproof casserole
whisk
measuring spoon
measuring cup
knife
3 qt. bowl
strainer

Chicken Madeira

Ingredients

Step One

4 boneless chicken breasts
2 oz. butter

Step Two

1/3 cup minced ham
1/2 cup grated Swiss cheese

Step Three

1 cup brown sauce

Step Four

1/3 cup madeira
2 Tablespoons tomato paste

Method

Melt butter and brown chicken in butter. Put chicken in oven proof casserole.

Either mince by hand or with a food processor fitted with a steel blade. Sprinkle ham and cheese over chicken.

Make one cup of brown sauce from prepackaged mix according to their directions.

Add madeira and tomato paste to brown sauce after the sauce has thickened. Mix well.

Step Five

Pour sauce over chicken and bake 35-40 minutes at 350°.

Step Six

1/2 # sliced mushrooms
1 Tablespoon butter

Using the same skillet, sauté mushrooms in butter until all moisture has been released and liquid evaporated. Sprinkle on top of chicken before serving.

Shopping List

4 boneless chicken breasts
3 oz. ham
3 oz. Swiss cheese
1 package brown sauce
1/3 cup madeira
2 Tablespoons tomato paste
1/2 # mushrooms
3 oz. butter

Utensils

skillet for browning chicken
    and cooking mushrooms
tongs
measuring cup
measuring spoons
1 quart saucepan
whisk
ovenproof casserole
knife to slice mushrooms
can opener for tomato paste
grater

Notes

Herb Chicken

Ingredients

Method

Step One

4 boneless chicken breasts

Remove skin and arrange in a single layer in a shallow baking dish.

Step Two

3 oz. butter

Melt butter and drizzle over chicken and bake for 20 minutes 350°.

Step Three

3/4 cup fine bread crumbs
1 Tablespoon fine minced onions
  or dried onion flakes
1/4 teaspoon garlic powder
2 Tablespoons minced dried parsley
1/2 teaspoon thyme
1 teaspoon rosemary*

While chicken is baking do Step Three. Mix ingredients together and when chicken has baked 20 minutes cover chicken with herb/crumb mixture.

If possible whirl rosemary in blender or use ground rosemary.

Step Four

1//2 cup dry vermouth

Pour vermouth around chicken and bake for 30 minutes at 350°.

*Hint: You can combine a larger amount of the herbs together and use a scant 3 Tablespoons of these mixed herbs per recipe. Store the extra in a jar to use another time.

May be served hot or cold
made ahead and refrigerated.
Tends to dry out if frozen.

Shopping List

4 chicken breasts boned
3 oz. butter
3/4 cup bread crumbs
1 Tablespoon minced dry onions
1/4 teaspoon garlic powder
2 Tablespoons minced dry parsley
1 teaspoon rosemary
1/2 teaspoon thyme
1/2 cup vermouth

Utensils

shallow baking dish
knife for mincing optional
measuring cup
measuring spoons
mixing bowl 2 cup size
tongs or spatula
saucepan to melt butter

Notes

Chicken Beauregard

Ingredients

Step One

2 boneless chicken breasts

Step Two

2 Tablespoons butter

Step Three

3 Tablespoons flour
6 oz. chicken broth

Step Four

1/2 cup dry vermouth
1½ teaspoon tarragon
1/4 cup half & half
2 Tablespoons grated parmesan cheese

Method

Remove skin and cut into finger size strips.

Melt butter in skillet large enough to hold chicken. Add chicken and lightly brown. Set aside in casserole.

Add flour to butter and make a roux stirring continually. Gradually add chicken broth whisking to mix smoothly. Be sure there are no lumps.

Add to Step Three and mix well. Pour over chicken in casserole.

Step Five

1/4 # sliced mushrooms
1 Tablespoon butter

Melt butter and sauté mushrooms until they have released all their liquid and moisture has evaporated. Put into chicken casserole mixing into sauce.

Step Six

2 Tablespoons grated parmesan cheese

Sprinkle on top of casserole. Bake at 350° for 20 minutes.

Shopping List

2 boneless chicken breasts
1/4 # mushrooms
1½ teaspoon terragon
1/2 cup dry vermouth
6 oz. (¾ cup) chicken broth
1/4 cup half and half
3 Tablespoons butter
1/4 cup grated parmesan cheese
Tablespoon flour

Utensils

knife
measuring spoons
measuring cup
skillet large enough to hold chicken
small pan for mushrooms
whisk
ovenproof casserole

Notes

Chicken Lausanne

Ingredients

Step One

2 boneless chicken breasts

Step Two

1 cup sweet vermouth
1 Tablespoon dijon mustard
1 cup beef broth

Step Three

1/2 # mushrooms sliced
2 Tablespoons butter

Step Four

3 Tablespoons butter
1/2 teaspoon tarragon

Method

Remove skin and cut into finger size strips. Set aside.

Mix together in bowl.

Sauté mushrooms in butter, in a skillet large enough to hold chicken, until all moisture has been released and liquid has evaporated. Set mushrooms aside with slotted spoon.

Melt butter in above skillet mix tarragon in and stir. Cook 1 minute.

Step Five

1/3 cup flour
salt/pepper

Put flour and seasonings in plastic bag. Add chicken and shake. Brown chicken in melted tarragon butter.

Step Six

Add vermouth mixture to chicken. Simmer uncovered 15 minutes. Add mushrooms simmer another 5 minutes. Cornstarch can be used to thicken sauce.

Shopping List

2 boneless chicken breasts
1 cup sweet vermouth
1 cup beef broth
1 Tablespoon dijon mustard
1/2 # mushrooms
5 Tablespoons butter
1/2 teaspoon tarragon
1/3 cup flour
salt/pepper

Utensils

plastic bag
knife
skillet large enough to hold chicken
tongs
measuring cup
measuring spoons
bowl

Notes

Chicken Sorrento

Ingredients

Step One

1 # mushrooms sliced
2 oz. butter

Step Two

6 boneless chicken breasts

Step Three

1 cup flour
1 Tablespoon curry powder
salt/pepper

Step Four

3 oz. butter

Method

Melt butter and sauté mushrooms until they have released their moisture and all liquid has evaporated.

Remove skin and cut chicken into finger length strips.

Mix together in plastic bag large enough to hold chicken. Put chicken in bag and coat well with flour mixture.

Melt butter in skillet large enough to hold chicken. Brown chicken.

Step Five

14 oz. chicken stock
1/2 cup Amaretto

Mix well in container. Add to chicken simmer 15 minutes.

Step Six

Can be made ahead and reheated but not as tasty that way. Serve with rice.

Thicken sauce with cornstarch if needed.

Shopping List

6 boneless chicken breasts
1 cup flour
1 Tablespoon curry
salt/pepper
3 oz. butter
14 oz. chicken stock
1/2 cup Amaretto

Utensils

knife
plastic bag large enough
   to hold chicken
can opener
measuring cup
measuring spoon
skillet large enough
   to hold chicken
bowl for sliced mushrooms

Notes

Chicken with Fresh Herbs

Ingredients

Step One

4 boneless chicken breasts

Step Two

2 oz. soft butter
1 Tablespoon basil
    or
1 Tablespoon tarragon

Step Three

Shopping List

4 boneless chicken breasts
2 oz. soft butter
basil
or
tarragon

Method

Mix butter and herb together. Slip butter between skin and meat or inject. Be careful not to rip skin completely off chicken.

Put chicken into shallow baking pan. Bake 45 minutes at 350°

Utensils

small bowl
wooden spoon
shallow baking dish
tong
measuring spoon

Herbed Chicken Breasts

For picnic or buffet

Ingredients

Method

Step One

6 chicken breasts with bone in
  or removed

Remove skin.

Step Two

1/2 teaspoon garlic powder
3 Tablespoons tarragon
3 Tablespoons dried minced parsley
3 Tablespoons dried minced chives
3 Tablespoons chervil
2 Tablespoons dry minced onions
6 Tablespoons fine bread crumbs

Mix together.

Step Three

4-6 Tablespoons butter

Rub butter onto chicken. Roll in
herbs. Bake at 350° for 40 minutes or
until done. Cool.

Shopping List

6 chicken breasts
garlic powder
tarragon
dry minced parsley
dry minced chives
chervil
dry minced onions
fine bread crumbs
4-6 oz. butter

Utensils

measuring spoon
knife
plate for herbs
ovenproof baking pan

Notes

Chicken Tandori

Ingredients

Step One

4 boneless chicken breasts

Step Two

Marinade

12 oz. yogurt plain
1 teaspoon ginger
1/4 teaspoon garlic powder
pinch red pepper
1/2 teaspoon ground cloves
1 teaspoon ground cinnamon
2 bay leaves
1 teaspoon salt

Step Three

Serve with curried rice

Method

Remove skin and cut into finger length strips.

Mix ingredients together. Marinate chicken over night.

Bake in casserole at 325° for 1 hour.

Shopping List

4 boneless chicken breasts
12 oz. plain yogurt
ginger
garlic powder
red pepper
ground cloves
ground cinnamon
2 bay leaves
salt

Utensils

knife
measuring spoon
measuring cup
bowl large enough to hold
  chicken and marinade
oven proof casserole

Notes

Lime Chicken

Ingredients

Step One

4 boneless chicken breasts
6 oz. can limeade
1/4 cup rum

Step Two

1/4 cup melted butter
1/2 teaspoon chervil
1 Tablespoon minced dry onion
1 teaspoon ground dill

Shopping List

4 boneless chicken breasts
6 oz. can limeade
1/4 cup rum
2 oz. butter
chervil
minced dry onion
ground dill

Method

Marinate chicken in baking dish 1 hour in limeade and rum.

Pour over chicken and bake at 400° for 35-45 minutes or until chicken is done.

Utensils

ovenproof casserole or baking dish
means to open limeade
measuring cup
measuring spoon
knife to cut butter

Cold Cornish Game Hens

Ingredients

Step One

4 game hens cut into quarters

Step Two

1½ teaspoons salt
1 teaspoon white pepper
1/2 teaspoon thyme
1/2 teaspoon oregano
1/4 teaspoon marjoram
1/2 teaspoon basil
1/4 teaspoon garlic powder

Step Three

6 Tablespoons butter

Step Four

3 oz. lemon juice
3 oz. honey
2 oz. sherry

Method

Have butcher cut hens in quarters. Arrange in ovenproof pan.

Put in blender on/off until blended fine.

Melt. Add all of Step One to melted butter. Pour over hens. Bake 10 mintes at 375°.

Heat in saucepan. Baste hens every 15 minutes for additional 30 minutes. Cool.

Shopping List

4 cornish game hens
salt
white pepper
thyme
oregano
basil
marjoram
garlic powder
6 Tablespoons butter
3 oz. lemon juice
3 oz. honey
2 oz. sherry

Utensils

ovenproof pan
electric blender
saucepan small
pastry brush for basting
tongs
measuring spoon
measuring cup

Notes

Turkey Kari

Ingredients

Step One

3 cups frozen diced onions
3 Tablespoons olive oil

Step Two

3-4 Tablespoons curry powder
3 Tablespoons flour

Step Three

3 cups rich chicken stock

Step Four

1/2 cup dry vermouth
1/3 cup raisins or currents
1 apple seeded and chopped
1/2 teaspoon thyme

Method

Cook slowly covered for 10 minutes.
Do not brown.

Add to Step One and cook slowly for 3
minutes.

Off heat pour into flour/onion mixture. Beat constantly with a whisk.
Return to heat.

Add all of Step Four to Step Three.

Step Five

1 cup coconut milk

Add slowly to Step Three and Four to thin.

Step Six

24 oz. cooked turkey meat

Cut into chunks. Put into sauce. Heat through either on top of stove or in oven.

This is an excellent dish to use the left over turkey from Thanksgiving. Serve with rice.

Condiments

cucumbers diced
green pepper diced
scallions
chutney
chopped peanuts
coconut shredded

Dice in food processor.

Shopping List

3 cups frozen diced onions
olive oil
1/4 cup curry powder
flour
2 cans rich chicken broth
1/2 cup dry vermouth
1/3 cup raisins or currents
1 apple
thyme
1 can coconut milk
24 oz. cooked turkey
shredded coconut

Utensils

measuring cup
measuring spoons
food processor for condiments
chef knife
large saucepan
knife
chopping board
oven casserole if cooked in oven
mitts
whisk
scale

Turkey Lasagna

Ingredients

Step One

10 oz. spinach noodles

Step Two

1/2 # mushrooms sliced
3 Tablespoons butter
1/2 cup diced frozen green pepper

Step Three

1¼ cup dry vermouth

Step Four

4 Tablespoons flour
4 Tablespoons butter

Step Five

4 cups half and half cream
1/2 teaspoon tarragon

Method

Cook in usual manner in salted water.

Sauté in butter 2-3 minutes.

Add Step Three to Step Two and reduce 1/4 cup. Set aside.

Melt butter and stir in flour cook 1-2 minutes.

Gradually whisk into roux to make a thick and creamy sauce. Add to Step Two.

Step Six

5 cups shredded cooked turkey
2 cups grated Swiss

Measure out and set aside.

Step Seven

1/2 cup slivered almonds

In bottom of pan put layer of spinach lasagna noodles. Then layer of turkey. Pour over some of the sauce - then sprinkle with cheese. Repeat these layers ending with cheese. Sprinkle on top. Bake at 350° for 40 minutes.

Shopping List

10 oz. spinach lasagna noodles
1/2 # mushrooms
7 Tablespoons butter
1/2 cup diced frozen green pepper
1¼ cup dry vermouth
4 Tablespoons butter
4 cups half & half cream
1/2 teaspoon tarragon
5 cups shredded cooked turkey
2 cups grated Swiss cheese
4 oz. slivered almonds

Utensils

large pot to cook lasagna noodles
knife
measuring spoons
measuring cups
whisk
2 bowls to hold turkey and cheese
lasagna pan
collander

Sour Cream Meatballs

Ingredients

Step One

1 # lean ground beef
1 teaspoon salt
2 Tablespoons minced dried onion
dash of pepper
pinch of cloves
pinch of nutmeg

Step Two

1/4 cup bread crumbs
6 oz. cream or milk
1 egg yolk beaten

Step Three

1-2 Tablespoons oil

Method

Mix together.

Soak bread crumbs in milk. Mix well with Step One.

Shape into small meatballs by rolling in palm of hand. Sauté in skillet a few at a time on all sides until brown. Roll around with slotted spoon. Reserve in bowl.

Step Four

1 can (14½ oz.) beef broth
roux

Reduce broth to 3/4 cup in saucepan.
Add premade roux to thicken.

Step Five

2/3 cup sour cream

Add to above over low heat. Return
meatballs to skillet. Spoon sauce over
it.

Shopping List

1 # lean ground meat
salt
dry minced onions
pepper
cloves
nutmeg
1/4 cup bread crumbs
6 oz. cream or milk
2 Tablespoons oil
1 can (14½ oz.) beef broth
roux
2/3 cup sour cream
1 egg

Utensils

skillet
slotted spoon
bowl
can opener
measuring cup
saucepan

Notes

Family Steak in Red Wine

Ingredients

Marinade

1/4 teaspoon allspice
1/4 teaspoon garlic powder
3 cups beaujolais
2 Tablespoons grated lemon peel
1 bay leaf
1 teaspoon thyme
1 teaspoon dried chives

Step One

olive oil
family steak

Step Two

marinade

Step Three

frozen sliced carrots
quartered peeled potato
frozen small onions
salt and pepper

Method

Marinate family steak at room temperature for 2 hours.

Brown meat in olive oil.

Pour marinade over meat and cook until barely tender.

Add all of Step Three to Step One and cook uncovered until vegetables are done. Add salt and pepper to taste.

Shopping List

2-3 # family steak
allspice ground
garlic powder
3 cups beaujolais
2 Tablespoons grated lemon peel
   (in bottle)
bay leaf
thyme
dried chives
olive oil
frozen sliced carrots
potatoes
frozen small onions
salt and pepper

Utensils

measuring spoons
measuring cups
wine bottle opener
knife
small dutch oven type pan
scissors

Notes

Marinated Family Steak

Ingredients

Step One

2 # round steak

Step Two

3/4 cup low salt soy sauce
1/3 cup water
1/3 cup sherry
1/2 teaspoon ground ginger

Shopping List

2 # round steak
6 oz. low salt soy sauce
1/3 cup sherry
ginger

Method

Put into pan in which it will fit snugly.

Combine the ingredients of Step Two in a jar or bowl and mix well. Pour over meat. Marinate at room temperature 2-3 hours or in refrigerator over night. Cook over charcoal or in a pan until medium rare. Slice thin.

Utensils

pan to hold steak
measuring cup
measuring spoon
charcoal grill or skillet to hold steak

Provençal Marinade for Beef

Ingredients

family steak
2 cups beaujolais wine
1/4 cup red wine vinegar
2 Tablespoons olive oil
3 cloves garlic unpeeled and cut in half
1 medium onion sliced
   or
6 Tablespoons minced dry onions
1 carrot sliced
1½ teaspoon salt

Method

Marinate 48 hours in refrigerator.

Add filled tea infuser to marinade.

Reserve marinade reduce over moderate heat by 1/3 then baste meat while grilling.

In Tea Infuser

1 bay leaf
2 allspice berries
3 peppercorns
1/4 teaspoon fennel seeds
1/4 teaspoon oregano
1/4 teaspoon thyme
1/4 teaspoon marjoram

Utensils

measuring cup
2 qt. container to mix ingredients
tea infuser
measuring spoon
knife
saucepan

Steak Cumberland Grilled

Ingredients

Step One

2 # family steak

Step Two

Marinade

1 cup tawny port
juice from orange
juice from 1/2 lemon
1 teaspoon dry mustard
1 teaspoon ginger
1 Tablespoon honey optional

Step Three

Method

Trimmed well by butcher.

Heat in saucepan to combine all ingredients well.

In a pan in which the meat will fit comfortably marinate meat 6 hours, turning a few times.

Remove meat from marinade and grill. In a saucepan reduce liquid by 1/3. When meat has been grilled remove to platter and pour sauce over meat.

Shopping List

2 # family steak
1 cup tawny port
1 orange
1/2 lemon
dry mustard
ginger
honey

Utensils

tongs
pan to hold meat while marinating
juicer
knife
measuring spoons
measuring cups
means to open jar and bottle
grill

Notes

Deviled Beef

Ingredients

Sauce

Step One

2 Tablespoons frozen chopped onions
1 Tablespoons dried minced chives
1/4 cup dry vermouth

Step Two

1/2 cup brown sauce

1 Tablespoon dijon style mustard

Step Three

1/3 cup heavy cream
pinch of white pepper

Serve over grilled beef

Method

Cook in saucepan and reduce to 2 Tablespoons. Set aside.

In a saucepan reduce brown sauce by 1/3.
Stir into brown sauce. Add wine/chive mixture.

Add to sauce.

Shopping List

beef for grilling of your choice
2 Tablespoons frozen chopped onions
1 Tablespoon dried minced chives
1/4 cup dry vermouth
1/2 cup brown sauce
dijon style mustard
1/3 cup heavy cream
white pepper

Utensils

2 small saucepans
measuring spoons
measuring cup
tongs
spoon
grill

Notes

Flemish Stew

Ingredients

Step One

2 # meat*
1 oz. butter or oil

Step Two

3 cups frozen diced onions
2 oz. butter

Step Three

1/4 teaspoon garlic powder
1 bay leaf
1/2 teaspoon thyme
2 Tablespoons dried parsley
1 Tablespoon cider vinegar
1 Tablespoon brown sugar
1 bottle DARK beer
1/2 cup beef stock
  (if canned dilute with water - equal
  parts water and stock.)

Method

Meat should be cubed in equal pieces. Pat dry with paper towels. Brown meat in butter. Transfer to oven proof casserole with tight fitting lid.

Thaw and pat dry.
Sauté onions until golden. Add to beef in casserole.

Combine all ingredients in skillet in which meat and onions were cooked. Scrape up brown nubbins, pour mixture over meat. Be sure lid fits tightly. Bake for 2 hours at 325°.

Step Four

roux

1. This stew can be made ahead and reheated.
2. Stew can be frozen.

Remove meat with a slotted spoon and thicken with roux, if needed. Return meat to sauce.

*See discussion of stew meat

Shopping List

2 # rump roast cut into cubes
3 oz. butter
3 cups frozen chopped onions
garlic powder
1 bay leaf
thyme
dried parsley
1 Tablespoon cider vinegar
1 Tablespoon brown sugar
1 bottle DARK beer
1 can beef broth

Utensils

knife if you cut up the meat
measuring spoon
measuring cup
skillet - large
casserole
   (ovenproof with tight fitting lid)

Notes

Pork Tenderloin - Grilled

Ingredients

2½ # - 3 # fresh pork tenderloin

Marinade

Step One

1/2 cup soy sauce
1/2 cup bourbon
1/4 cup molasses or other sweetening
   of your choice

Mustard Sauce

1/2 cup sour cream
1/2 cup mayonnaise
2 Tablespoons dried onion flakes
2 teaspoons white wine vinegar
1 Tablespoon dry mustard

Grill Pork

Serve with mustard sauce.

Method

Mix in a dish that will hold pork - like a long loaf pan. Marinate 4-6 hours.

Make a day ahead.

Mix together and refrigerate.

Shopping List

2½-3 # pork tenderloin
1/2 cup soy sauce
1/2 cup bourbon
1/4 cup molasses or other sweetening
1/2 cup sour cream
1/2 cup mayonnaise
2 Tablespoons dried onion flakes
2 teaspoons white wine vinegar
1 Tablespoon dry mustard

Utensils

grill
tongs
measuring cup
measuring spoons
bowl for sauce
container to marinate pork

Notes

Creole Pork Chops

Ingredients

Step One

2 pork chops cut 1" thick
small amount of oil

Step Two

1/2 cup frozen chopped onions
1/2 cup frozen chopped peppers
1/8 teaspoon garlic powder
1 Tablespoon butter

Step Three

3/4 cup Italian tomatoes roughly cut
1/4 cup sweet vermouth
1/2 teaspoon oregano
1/4 teaspoon basil

Method

In skillet large enough to hold chops brown in oil for 5 minutes per side. Remove chops from pan and put on plate.

In above unwashed skillet sauté in butter until pepper becomes soft and onions translucent. Approximately 5 minutes.

Mix all ingredients of Step Three together and pour into skillet in which onions and peppers have been cooking. Simmer about 20 minutes. Add pork chops and simmer an additional 25 minutes.

Shopping List

2 pork chops
1/2 cup frozen chopped onions
1/4 cup chopped peppers
garlic powder
oil
1 Tablespoon butter
1 small can Italian tomatoes
1/4 cup sweet vermouth
oregano
basil

Utensils

skillet
mixing bowl
tongs
fork
measuring cup
measuring spoon
plate for pork chops
spoon

Notes

Chili

Ingredients

Method

Step One

1/2 # ground beef

Brown meat and crumble. Drain in collander then put in large saucepan.

Step Two

2/3 cup frozen chopped onions

Thaw and add to meat.

Step Three

1 can (10½ oz.) tomato soup
1 can (25 oz.) whole peeled tomatoes
   cut in half
1 can (10½ oz.) tomato sauce
2½ teaspoon chili powder
3/4 teaspoon cumin
1/4 teaspoon cayenne pepper
1 can (25 oz.) kidney beans
   DRAINED

Add all ingredients of Step Three to meat and onions. Simmer 30-40 minutes slowly uncovered.

CAREFUL NOT TO SCORCH

Shopping List

1/2 # ground beef
2/3 cup frozen chopped onions
25 oz. can whole peeled tomatoes
10½ oz. can tomato sauce
10½ oz. can tomato soup
chili powder
cumin
cayenne pepper
25 oz. can kidney beans

Utensils

spatula
skillet
3-4 qt. saucepan
large spoon
can opener
measuring cup
measuring spoon

Notes

Eggplant and Canadian Bacon with Eggs

Ingredients	Method

Step One

1 eggplant salt	Peel and slice into 8 slices. Sprinkle eggplant with salt and let stand 1 hour in collander.

Step Two

1/4 cup olive oil	Heat oil and brown eggplant. Put in ovenproof container and set in warm oven.

Step Three

8 slices of Canadian bacon	Brown Canadian bacon and put on top of eggplant.

Step Four

8 eggs	Fry eggs sunnyside up and put on top of Canadian bacon. Serve with tomato sauce and parmesan cheese.

Shopping List

1 eggplant
1/4 cup olive oil
8 slices Canadian bacon
8 eggs
salt
parmesan cheese
ingredients for tomato sauce

Utensils

knife
peeler
large skillet
ovenproof pan or plate
platter
spatula
collander

Notes

Tomato Sauce for Eggplant and Canadian Bacon

Ingredients

1 can (16 oz.) tomato bits in sauce
1/4 cup sweet vermouth
1 Tablespoon basil
1 Tablespoon oregano
1/8 teaspoon garlic powder
salt and pepper as needed

Method

Mix well. Cook uncovered over low heat letting sauce reduce to thicken.

Utensils

can opener
measuring cup
measuring spoon
1 qt. sauce pan

Lamb Stew

Ingredients

Step One

2½ # lamb shoulder cut in 1" cubes

Step Two

1/4 cup flour
1 teaspoon dry mustard
1/4 teaspoon ground celery seed
1 teaspoon thyme

Step Three

2-3 Tablespoons bacon drippings

Step Four

1 cup frozen chopped onions
1/2 cup dry vermouth
2 cups beef broth

Method

Step One

Have your butcher cut up the lamb. Do NOT use lamb stew meat.

Step Two

Combine in a plastic or paper bag all of Step Two. Put lamb in bag in small amounts. Shake gently covering lamb well with seasoned flour.

Step Three

Brown meat in bacon drippings. Remove with slotted spoon to oven proof casserole with cover.

Step Four

Brown in pan in which meat was browned. Pour vermouth into pan getting up all the brown nubbins with a wooded spoon. Pour beef broth into skillet mix with wine and onions then pour over lamb.

Step Five

4 carrots sliced diagonally
3 potatoes cut in wedges

Add all of Step Five to the casserole. Bake covered in a 350° oven for 1 hour. Remove cover and continue baking for 20 minutes - reducing the liquid. Serve with crunchy bread.

Shopping List

2½ # lamb shoulder cut up
1/4 cup flour
dry mustard
ground celery seed
thyme
bacon drippings
1/4 cup dry vermouth
2 cups beef broth
4 carrots
3 potatoes
8 oz. frozen chopped onions

Utensils

slotted spoon
skillet
knife
peeler
measuring spoons
measuring cup
wooden spoon
plastic or paper bag
can opener
ovenproof casserole

Notes

Zucchini and Lamb Casserole

Ingredients

Step One

3 Tablespoons tomato paste
3 cups water
1 cup uncooked long grain rice
1 teaspoon cinnamon
salt and pepper

Step Two

6 small zucchini sliced 1/4"

Step Three

1 # ground lamb

Step Four

Method

Mix together all of Step One.

Lay zucchini in bottom of casserole.

Brown in skillet - breaking up the lumps. Drain in strainer. Then put on top of zucchini.

Pour tomato mixture over zucchini and lamb. Bake at 350° for 25 minutes or until done.

Shopping List

3 Tablespoons tomato paste
1 cup long grain rice
cinnamon
salt and pepper
6 small zucchini
1 # ground lamb

Utensils

measuring spoons
measuring cups
medium size casserole
1 qt. container to mix liquid
spatula
knife
skillet
strainer
can opener
bowl in which to strain lamb

Notes

Poached Salmon with Dill Sauce

Ingredients

Step One

1 Tablespoon butter
4 salmon steaks or fillets
1 cup dry vermouth

Step Two

Method

Put salmon in a buttered baking dish in which it will fit comfortably. Pour vermouth over the salmon. Bake covered with foil approximately 20 minutes at 350° depending upon the thickness of the salmon. Do not let it dry out.

If it is to be served cold - chill in a dish in the refrigerator. If it is to be served hot bake at last minute. Remove from baking dish and arrange on a platter or individual plate.

Shopping List

4 salmon steaks or fillets
1 cup dry vermouth
1 Tablespoon butter
4 Tablespoons white WINE vinegar
2 Tablespoons sugar
1/4 cup dijon style mustard
1 cup mayonnaise
4 Tablespoons dry dill weed

Utensils

baking dish for salmon
measuring cup
knife
measuring spoon
1 qt. mixing bowl
1 bowl large enough to hold
    mayonnaise and mustard

Dill Sauce

Ingredients

Step One

4 Tablespoons white wine vinegar
2 Tablespoons sugar

Step Two

1/4 cup dijon style mustard
1 cup mayonnaise
4 Tablespoons dry dill weed

Sauce keeps well in refrigerator for week to ten days.

Method

Put vinegar in 1 qt. bowl. Sprinkle sugar into vinegar mixing to dissolve.

Mix together then mix in with vinegar and sugar. Mix dill weed in with mayonnaise well and chill.

Notes

Side Dishes

Side Dishes

Artichokes

Ingredients

Step One

whole artichokes

Step Two

Step Three

Method

Step One

Remove a few of the lower leaves then cut off the stem so artichoke will sit flat.

Step Two

If you are able cut off the top 1/2" of the artichoke.

Step Three

Put artichokes in a steamer and steam until second leaf from base pulls out easily.

To test, I remove the top of the steamer from the steam pot and set on a dish towel. YOU CAN GET A STEAM BURN if you test artichokes in a steamer.

Serve artichoke either cold or hot with melted butter or mayonnaise.

When eating an artichoke, as you get down to the choke, remember to scrape away with a spoon the fine hairs on the choke. It pulls away quite easily. You do NOT want to eat those fine hairs.

Shopping List

whole artichokes

Utensils

knife
pan large enough to hold artichokes
dishtowel

Notes

Minted Peas

Ingredients

Step One

frozen peas
peppermint
butter

Method

Melt butter in skillet. Add a few drops of extract. Pour in frozen peas and stirfry 1-2 minutes. Serve immediately.

Shopping List

frozen peas
peppermint
butter

Utensils

skillet
wooden spoon

Notes

Almond Peas

Ingredients

Step One

frozen peas
almond extract
butter

Shopping List

frozen peas
almond extract
butter

Method

Melt butter in skillet. Add a few drops of extract. Pour in frozen peas and stirfry 1-2 minutes. Serve immediately.

Utensils

skillet
wooden spoon

Notes

String Beans

Ingredients

Step One

string beans

Step Two

sliced mushrooms, canned or fresh
butter

Step Three

Method

Steam beans until barely al dente.

Sauté in butter until fresh mushrooms have released their juices and all moisture has evaporated.

Add string beans to mushrooms and butter and stir fry until al dente.

Shopping List

string beans
sliced mushrooms, canned or fresh
butter

Utensils

steamer
skillet
wooden spoon

Rice

Cooking rice can be tiresome if you are doing nothing else in the kitchen. If you are sitting in another room while the rice is cooking, the rice more often than not gets burned because you forget it. I have more than once cooked rice for two hundred people, every kernel with a lovely texture, and then come home and cooked rice for two which I duly scorched or burned. I then devised the following method to allow me and the rice to enjoy our evening.

If you normally cook for two people then make enough rice for eight. Package the rice in two person servings and freeze it. When you wish to serve the rice fit a strainer, large enough to hold the rice, over a saucepan of simmering water. Put the rice in the strainer and cover with aluminum foil. Occasionally separate the kernels of rice with a fork. When the rice is heated through it is then ready to serve. This method can be used with long grain, brown and wild rice.

Portions of raw rice for the average eater are the following: 2 persons = 1/2 cup raw rice. If you are serving a large group, 5 persons = 1 cup raw rice.

Wild Rice Casserole

Ingredients

Step One

1/4 # wild rice

Step Two

1 can (14 ½ oz.) chicken broth
4 oz. water

Step Three

1 Tablespoon butter
1/4 cup long grain rice
1/4 cup frozen chopped onions
1/4 cup chopped walnuts or pecans

Step Four

1/2 # mushrooms
2 Tablespoons butter

Method

Soak wild rice in water 30 minutes, then drain in strainer.

Bring broth and water to a boil. Add wild rice. Cook 20 minutes.

Melt butter and cook all of Step Three in butter 1-2 minutes. When wild rice has cooked 20 minutes add Step Three to the wild rice and cook an additional 15 minutes.

Slice mushrooms either by hand or with food processor. Sauté mushrooms in melted butter until mushrooms have released all their liquid and moisture has evaporated. Set aside.

Step Five

1 cup frozen peas
salt and pepper

Thaw peas. Put rice and mushrooms in ovenproof casserole. Add peas. Toss to mix. Season with salt and pepper.

Make ahead and reheat covered with foil in a 350° oven until heated through.

Shopping List

1/4 # wild rice
1 can (14 ½ oz.) chicken broth
3 Tablespoons butter
1/4 cup long grain rice
1/4 cup frozen chopped onions
1/4 cup chopped walnuts or pecans
1/2 # mushrooms
8 oz. frozen peas
salt and pepper

Utensils

bowl to soak rice
strainer to drain rice
saucepan large enough
   to hold all ingredients
measuring cup
measuring spoon
knife
skillet to cook mushrooms
ovenproof casserole
food processor, optional

Notes

Wild Rice

Ingredients

Step One

1/4 # wild rice

Step Two

14 oz. chicken broth home made
  or canned
water

Shopping List

1/4 # wild rice
14 oz. chicken broth

Method

Step One

Soak in warm-hot water 30-40 minutes, drain.

Step Two

Put rice in saucepan, cover with chicken broth so the broth is above rice by 2". Add water if necessary. Cook slowly covered for 20-30 minutes until grain has just about popped. Put rice in strainer over pot of simmering water. Cover with foil. Steam 10 minutes or until grains have popped.

Utensils

saucepan
strainer
aluminum foil
spoon
can opener

Baked Rice

Ingredients

Step One

1 qt. milk
1 cup raw grain rice
1 teaspoon salt

Step Two

1/2 cup sugar
1 teaspoon vanilla

Step Three

3 egg yolks
3 egg whites

Step Four

1 Tablespoon butter

Method

Cook in double boiler 1¼ hours until almost all milk is absorbed.

Add sugar and vanilla to Step One.

Lightly beat yolks, add to Step One. Beat egg whites until soft peaks form. Fold into Step One.

Butter a 6 cup soufflé dish. Pour in rice mixture. Bake at 350° for 30 minutes until puffed and golden.

Shopping List

1 qt. milk
1 cup raw long grain rice
1 teaspoon salt
1/2 cup sugar
1 teaspoon vanilla
3 eggs
1 Tablespoon butter

Utensils

measuring cup
measuring spoons
battery powered beater
   or electric mixer
double boiler
small bowl to beat yolks
6 cup soufflé dish
bowl to beat egg whites

Notes

Zucchini/Tomato/Onion Casserole

Ingredients

Step One

3 zucchini
Beau Monde seasoning
pepper

Method

Slice zucchini either by hand or with food processor 1/4" thick. Put in bottom of casserole. Sprinkle lightly with Beau Monde and pepper.

Step Two

1 Tablespoon butter

Dot zucchini with butter.

Step Three

3 tomatoes
Beau Monde seasoning
pepper
1 teaspoon basil

Slice tomatoes 1/4" thick put on top of zucchini sprinkle lightly with Beau Monde, pepper and basil.

Step Four

3/4 cup diced frozen onion, thawed
2 Tablespoons frozen chopped chives

Pat onion dry. Sprinkle onion and chives on top of tomatoes.

Step Five

Bake at 350° for 30 minutes.

Step Six

4 oz. sliced American cheese

Put sliced American cheese on top of casserole continue baking 10 minutes.

May be assembled ahead
and refrigerated.

Shopping List

3 zucchini
3 tomatoes
3/4 cup diced frozen onions
2 Tablespoons frozen chopped chives
1 teaspoon basil
1 Tablespoon butter
Beau Monde seasoning
pepper
4 oz. sliced American cheese

Utensils

casserole
knife
food processor, optional
measuring cup
measuring spoon

Notes

Zucchini Boats with Onions and Parmesan

Ingredients

Step One

3 large zucchini

Step Two

3 cups frozen diced onions
3 Tablespoons butter
salt and pepper

Step Three

4 oz. parmesan cheese

Method

Step One

Cut in half lengthwise. Hollow the zucchini out carefully with a spoon or knife. Do NOT pierce the skin. Chop pulp and reserve.

Step Two

Sauté onions in a skillet in butter until translucent. Add chopped zucchini to onions. Cook 5 minutes. Season with salt and pepper.

Step Three

Spoon zucchini/onion mixture into zucchini boats. Top boats with parmesan. Put filled boats in shallow baking pan. Bake at 350° for 25 minutes.

Shopping List

3 large zucchini
3 cups frozen diced onions
3 Tablespoons butter
4 oz. parmesan cheese
salt and pepper

Utensils

knife
spoon
spatula
measuring cups
skillet
shallow baking dish

Notes

Glazed Carrots

Ingredients

Step One

18 oz. carrots

Step Two

4 oz. butter
1/3 cup brown sugar
   or
1/4 cup honey
3 oz. carrots per person

Freezes well.

Shopping List

18 oz. carrots
4 oz. butter
1/3 cup brown sugar
   or
1/4 cup honey

Method

Peel and slice into 1" chunks. Parboil until al dente or steam.

Melt butter in skillet large enough to hold carrots. Mix in brown sugar until sugar is well blended with butter. Add drained carrots to butter. Stir carrots around, coating well.

Utensils

vegetable peeler
knife
saucepan large enough
   to hold carrots
skillet
spoon

Tomatoes Provençal

Ingredients

Step One

6 whole slightly underripe
  firm tomatoes

Step Two

6 oz. bread crumbs
1/2 teaspoon parsley
1/4 teaspoon thyme
1/2 teaspoon basil
1/4 cup grated parmesan cheese

Do not cook ahead.

Do not freeze.

May be assembled ahead.

Shopping List

6 whole tomatoes
6 oz. bread crumbs
parsley
thyme
basil
1/4 cup grated parmesan cheese

Method

Cut in half. Flick seeds out with a spoon. Do not remove much of the tomato. Put tomato on baking sheet.

Mix together, sprinkle over 12 tomato halves. Bake at 375° for 10 minutes or until tomatoes start to cook and are not mushy and bread crumbs are golden. Serve immediately.

Utensils

sharp knife to cut tomatoes
spoon
measuring spoon
measuring cup
shallow baking sheet

Ratatouille

Ingredients

Method

Step One

2 eggplant
salt

Cut into wedges then slice 1/4" thick in processor. Set aside in collander. Salt eggplant.

Step Two

4 medium onions

Cut in wedges slice in processor. Set aside.

Step Three

8 green peppers
10 small zucchini

Quarter, remove seeds from pepper. Slice zucchini and pepper in food processor. Set aside.

Step Four

3 medium cans Italian tomatoes

Slice in half. Reserve juice perhaps for gazpacho soup. It will not be needed in this recipe.

Assembling the Ratatouille

Step One

1/4 cup olive oil
1/4 cup corn oil
3/4 garlic powder

Serve either hot or cold.

Pour oil into large baking pan with deep sides. Put the vegetables in the pan by layers starting with:
    onions
    green peppers
    eggplant
    zucchini
    tomatoes
    garlic
Cook over low heat simmering with cover for 20 minutes. Stir vegetables and continue cooking uncovered for an additional 20 minutes.

Shopping List

2 eggplant
4 medium onions
8 green peppers
10 small zucchini
3 medium cans Italian tomatoes
1/4 cup olive oil
1/4 cup corn oil
3/4 teaspoon garlic powder

Utensils

food processor
knife
collander
can opener
baking pan with high sides
wooden spoon
measuring cup
measuring spoon
aluminum foil

Vegetables

I am really a firm believer that the tastiest vegetables are absolutely fresh. The best way I think to cook them is in a steamer. Vegetables can be enhanced by herbs so turn yourself loose with herbs and learn how you like it best. If you happen to have a little herb garden all the better - a little snip of fresh herbs does wonders to any meal. Vegetables add color to a meal so *please* think about that when you are planning your menu. Serving a white fish, cauliflower and rice on a white plate is not very appetizing.

When you are purchasing vegetables do look at their color and firmness. Here are a few examples of what to look for. Cauliflower should be white with no brown spots. Broccoli should be green with no yellow spots. Both should be firm. Asparagus with a large amount of white on the end means a lot of wastage for you. You will be paying a premium price for what will get thrown out in the garbage.

If you keep your knife sharp you will be able to cut the vegetables quite easily. However a dull knife will definitely put strain on your joints.

Salads

Salads

String Beans Marinated

Ingredients

Step One

1½ # string beans
salt

Step Two

4 oz. vinaigrette

Shopping List

1½ # string beans
4 oz. vinaigrette
salt

Served cold
Variations

Method

Remove stems and any large strings from fresh string beans. Boil in salted water until al dente. Drain well in collander.

Put beans into bowl pour vinaigrette over beans while they are still hot. Cool to room temperature. Then chill. Should be made 6 hours in advance.

Utensils

knife
saucepan in which to cook beans
collander
measuring cup
bowl large enough to hold beans

Add your favorite herbs to the warm beans and pour vinaigrette over.

Marinated Vegetables

Ingredients

Step One

12 oz. broccoli buds
6 oz. cauliflower

Step Two

12 oz. carrots

6-8 oz. mushrooms

Step Three

Italian salad dressing
or vinaigrette

Step Four

6-8 cherry tomatoes

The broccoli, cauliflower and carrots
can be parboiled for 2 minutes, drained
and the dressing added while still hot.

Method

Very coarsely chopped

Peel and thinly slice with aid of food
processor.
Slice either by hand or with food processor.

Pour over vegetables and refrigerate a
few hours.

Before serving, cut tomatoes in half
and add to vegetables.

Shopping List

1 large bunch broccoli
1/2 head of cauliflower
12 oz. carrots
1/2 # mushrooms
6-8 cherry tomatoes
Italian or vinaigrette dressing

Utensils

knife
food processor
vegetable peeler
bowl for vegetables
saucepan, optional
collander, optional

Notes

Tomato-Cucumber-Basil Salad

Ingredients

Step One

3 large ripe tomatoes

Step Two

1½ medium cucumbers
salt

Step Three

6 fresh basil leaves
1/3 cup vinaigrette

Method

Slice medium, thickly. Put into serving bowl.

Peel and slice thinly with aid of food processor. Put in a collander and salt. Drain. When well drained, add to tomatoes.

Roughly chop leaves, add to vinaigrette and pour over tomatoes and cucumbers. Chill for a few hours.

Shopping List

3 large ripe tomatoes
1½ medium cucumbers
6 fresh basil leaves
1/3 cup vinaigrette
salt

Utensils

knife
food processor, optional
vegetable peeler
collander
measuring cup
serving bowl

Notes

Cucumber Yogurt Salad

Ingredients

Step One

2 medium cucumbers
salt

Step Two

1/3 cup yogurt
1/3 cup sour cream
Beau Monde
1 teaspoon dill weed

Delicious served with cold salmon

Shopping List

2 medium cucumbers
salt
1/3 cup yogurt
1/3 cup sour cream
Beau Monde seasoning
1 teaspoon dill weed

Method

If peels are thick, remove them. Slice in a food processor and then put in a collander. Sprinkle with salt and let drain 1 hour. Then continue draining on paper towels.

Mix together in a bowl and then mix in drained cucumber slices.

Utensils

food processor
collander
knife
bowl
paper towels
measuring cups
measuring spoons

Cucumber Salad

Ingredients

Step One

24 oz. cucumbers

Step Two

4 oz. sour cream
4 oz. mayonnaise
1 teaspoon dill weed
1/2 teaspoon Beau Monde seasoning
salt/pepper

Cucumbers can be sliced, drained and stored covered 1 day ahead. Do not mix with dressing until shortly before being served.

Method

Peel cucumbers and slice thinly either by hand or with processor. Salt and drain for 1 hour in collander. Remove and place on paper towel to dry.

Mix together well in a bowl large enough to hold the cucumbers. Add the cucumbers just before serving.

Shopping List

24 oz. cucumbers
4 oz. sour cream
4 oz. mayonnaise
dill weed
Beau Monde seasoning
salt/pepper

Utensils

medium sized bowl
vegetable peeler
food processor, optional
collander
paper towels
measuring spoon
measuring cup
knife

Notes

Layered Salad

Ingredients	Method
Step One	
head lettuce	Shred lettuce and put in bottom of glass serving bowl.
Step Two	
2 cups sliced celery	Slice either by hand or with food processor. Sprinkle on top of lettuce.
Step Three	
3 cups frozen peas	Thaw peas, do not cook. Sprinkle on top of celery
Step Four	
thinly sliced onion rings	Slice enough for one thin layer.
Step Five	
2 cups sliced water chestnuts	Sprinkle over onions.

Step Six

1 cup diced hard cooked eggs

Dice by hand or with egg slicer. Sprinkle over onions.

Step Seven

1/2 - 3/4 cup bacon bits

Sprinkle on top of eggs.

Step Eight

3/4-1 cup mayonnaise

Frost top with mayonnaise. Cover tightly with plastic wrap. Refrigerate over night.

Shopping List

1 head lettuce
8 stalks celery
3 cups frozen peas
1 small - medium onion
2 cups sliced water chestnuts
6 hard cooked eggs
1/2 - 3/4 cup real bacon bits
3/4-1 cup mayonnaise

Utensils

saucepan
glass serving bowl
sharp knife
food processor, optional
egg slicer that will
   slice both ways
measuring cup
spoon
spatula (plastic)

Herbed Cottage Cheese

Ingredients

Step One

12 oz. sour cream
4 Tablespoons frozen chopped onions
2 Tablespoons frozen chopped chives

Step Two

2 Tablespoons summer savory
2 Tablespoons tarragon
2 Tablespoons basil

Step Three

2 pounds cottage cheese

Hint: If this turns out to be a favorite dish, make a large batch of herbs in blender and store them in a jar.

Method

Thaw onions and chives. Mix them in a bowl with sour cream.

In an electric blender, put savory, tarragon and basil. Whirl on/off in blender until fine. Add to Step One and mix well.

Add cottage cheese to sour cream mixture. Stir well. Refrigerate overnight before serving.

Shopping List

12 oz. sour cream
1/4 cup or 4 Tablespoons
   frozen chopped onions
2 Tablespoons frozen chopped chives
summer savory
tarragon
basil
2 pounds cottage cheese

Utensils

3 qt. bowl or larger
measuring spoons
measuring cup
spoon
electric blender

Notes

Curried Turkey Salad

Ingredients

Step One

12 oz. cooked turkey

Step Two

2 stalks celery
salt and pepper

Step Three

5 oz. curried mayonnaise

To Serve

a bed of lettuce
cherry tomatoes, cut in half
sweet gherkins, cut in quarters
sliced hard cooked eggs
black olives

Method

In food processor fitted with a metal blade, using on/off pulse dice turkey. Put in bowl.

Dice in food processor. Add to turkey.

Mix in with turkey and celery.

Shopping List

12 oz. cooked turkey
5 oz. mayonnaise
oil
curry
2 stalks celery
1 head leaf lettuce
8 cherry tomatoes
4 sweet gherkins
3 hard cooked eggs
8 black olives, pitted
salt and pepper

Utensils

large bowl
spatula
knife
food processor
egg slicer
measuring cup
platter

Notes

Chicken Salad

Ingredients

Step One

24 oz. cooked chicken

Step Two

4 stalks celery

Step Three

7-8 oz. mayonnaise
2 teaspoon celery seed
Beau Monde seasoning
1 teaspoon minced dry onions
1 teaspoon minced dry chives

To Serve

bed of lettuce
cherry tomatoes, cut in half
peeled cucumbers, cut in quarters
hard cooked eggs, sliced
slices of pimento
black olives
artichoke hearts

Method

Dice cooked chicken in food processor. Put in bowl.

Dice in food processor and add to chicken.

Mix together well, then add to chicken and celery.

173

Shopping List

24 oz. cooked chicken
4 stalks celery
1 cup mayonnaise
celery seed
Beau Monde seasoning
minced dry onions
minced dry chives
leaf lettuce
cherry tomatoes
1 cucumber
3 eggs
1 small jar pimento
1 small can pitted black olives
1 small can artichoke hearts

Utensils

large bowl
knife
food processor
measuring spoons
measuring cup
vegetable peeler
spatula
small bowl
can opener
means to open jar

Notes

Italian Beef Salad

Ingredients

Step One

1/2 # cooked and thinly
  sliced roast beef
1/2 cup Italian dressing

Step Two

1/4 cup Italian dressing
1/2 # thinly sliced mushrooms

Step Three

3/4 cup Italian dressing
1/4 teaspoon basil
1/8 teaspoon oregano

Step Four

2 teaspoon minced dry chives
1/4 cup sliced ripe olives
2 teaspoon diced pimento
1/2 # frozen uncooked peas

Method

Marinate beef in Italian dressing 3-4 hours.

Marinate mushrooms in dressing. Do not marinate with beef.

Mix together and set aside.

Step Five

1½ cups long grain rice

Cook and drain. While warm, mix with Step Three. Chill, then add beef, chives, olives, pimento, mushrooms and peas. Mix well.

Shopping List

1/2 # cooked and thinly
sliced roast beef
1½ cups Italian dressing
1/2 # sliced mushrooms
basil
oregano
minced dry chives
1 small can pitted ripe olives
1 small jar diced pimento
8 oz. frozen peas
1½ cups long grain rice

Utensils

4 cereal size bowls
measuring spoons
measuring cups
knife
spoon and fork

Notes

Cucumber Molded Salad

Ingredients

Step One

2 large cucumbers

Step Two

1 Tablespoon unflavored gelatin
2 Tablespoons lemon juice

Step Three

2 cups boiling water
2 teaspoons salt

Step Four

2 teaspoons minced dry onions
2 cups sour cream
2 teaspoons dill weed
1/2 cup mayonnaise
1 teaspoon Beau Monde seasoning

Method

Peel, then grate with a food processor.
Drain well on paper towels.

Dissolve gelatin in lemon juice.

Mix gelatin in water and salt. Chill
until slightly thickened.

Mix well in a bowl, then fold into
thickened gelatin.

Step Five

Fold in drained cucumbers. Oil ring mold and pour in cucumber mixture. Chill overnight.

Shopping List

2 large cucumbers
1 pkg. unflavored gelatin
1 lemon
salt
2 teaspoons dry minced onions
16 oz. sour cream
dill weed
1/2 cup mayonnaise
Beau Monde seasoning
oil

Utensils

vegetable peeler
collander to drain cucumbers
grater or food processor
small bowl
large bowl
spatula
measuring spoon
measuring cup
paper towels
ring mold

Notes

Spicy Peach Mold

Ingredients

Step One

2 1 # cans sliced cling peaches

Step Two

1/2 cup vinegar
1½ cup peach syrup
1 cup sugar
24 whole cloves
1/4 teaspoon cinnamon

Step Three

6 oz. orange gelatin
1½ cup cold water

Method

Drain peaches RESERVING liquid. Chop coarsely.

In a saucepan, bring to boil. Simmer 20 minutes, remove cloves. Liquid should measure 2 cups. Add water if not enough.

Add gelatin to hot liquid of Step Two and dissolve. Mix cold water and chopped peaches. Pour into small sized baking pan. Chill. Cut into squares and serve with ham or garnish the ham.

Shopping List

2 cans (1 #) sliced cling peaches
1/2 cup vinegar
1 cup sugar
24 whole cloves
cinnamon
6 oz. orange gelatin

Utensils

can opener
strainer
2 medium bowls
measuring cup
saucepan
measuring spoon
small baking pan

Notes

Vegetable Mold

Ingredients

Step One

6 oz. lemon gelatin
1/2 cup boiling water

Step Two

1/4 cup Italian dressing
1½ cups cold water

Step Three

1 cup sliced zucchini
1 cup cucumber, peeled and sliced
1/2 cup grated carrots

Method

Dissolve gelatin in boiling water.

Stir into gelatin the dressing and cold water. Chill until slightly thickened.

While gelatin is thickening, prepare the vegetables. Quarter and slice by hand the zucchini. Peel the cucumber and slide in food processor. Grate the carrot with food processor. Drain and pat dry the cucumbers with a paper towel. Fold all vegetables into gelatin mixture and chill until firm.

Shopping List

6 oz. lemon gelatin
1/4 cup Italian dressing
2 small zucchini
2 small cucumbers
1 carrot

Utensils

large bowl
saucepan
measuring cup
food processor
paper towels
knife
wooden spoon
vegetable peeler

Notes

Spinach Salad Mold

Ingredients

Step One

10 oz. frozen chopped spinach

Step Two

4 oz. sour cream
1/2 cup frozen chopped onions
1/2 cup chopped water chestnuts
1 teaspoon lemon juice
1 teaspoon chopped dried parsley
1 teaspoon tarragon
1 teaspoon salt

Step Three

1 Tablespoon gelatin, unflavored
1/4 cup cold water

Step Four

3¾ cups hot water

Method

Drain and cook spinach dry. Set aside.

Chop water chestnuts roughly by hand. Mix all ingredients of Step Two together in a large bowl.

Soften gelatin in cold water.

Dissolve in hot water, mix in with sour cream and spinach. Chill in oiled mold.

Shopping List

10 oz. frozen chopped spinach
4 oz. sour cream
1/2 cup frozen chopped onions
1 can (5-6 oz.) water chestnuts
1 teaspoon lemon juice
dried parsley
tarragon
salt
1 pkg. unflavored gelatin
oil

Utensils

skillet
measuring cup
knife or food processor
large bowl
small bowl
wooden spoon
measuring spoons
mold

Notes

Ham Mousse

Ingredients

Step One

1/2 # boiled ham
1/2 # cooked Virginia ham
1/4 cup sweet pickle relish

Step Two

2 Tablespoons gelatin
1/4 cup cold chicken broth

Step Three

3/4 cup hot chicken broth

Step Four

2 Tablespoons mayonnaise

Step Five

6 egg whites

Method

Mince ham by food processor. Drain pickle relish well then mix with ham. Put into a 2 qt. bowl.

Soften gelatin in chicken broth in 2 cup container.

Pour into Step Two and dissolve gelatin in hot broth.

Add Step Three and Four to Step One.

Beat until stiff.

Step Six

1/2 cup whipping cream

Beat until stiff. Fold Step Five and Six into ham mixture. Chill overnight.

Shopping List

1/2 # boiled ham
1/2 # cooked Virginia ham
1/4 cup sweet pickle relish
2 Tablespoons gelatin
1 cup chicken broth
2 Tablespoons mayonnaise
6 egg whites
1/2 cup whipping cream

Utensils

food processor
measuring cup
means to open jar
measuring spoon
scissors
can opener
small bowl (2)
2 qt. mixing bowl
electric mixer and bowls

Notes

Pineapple Sour Cream Mold

Ingredients

Step One

6 oz. lemon Jell-o
1/2 Tablespoon unflavored gelatin
1 teaspoon salt
2 cups boiling water

Step Two

1/2 cup cold water
2 Tablespoons lemon juice
2 cups sour cream

Step Three

3 cups crushed well-drained pineapple

Shopping List

6 oz. lemon Jell-o
1 pkg. unflavored gelatin
salt
2 Tablespoons lemon juice
2 cups sour cream
2 cans (14 ½ oz.) crushed pineapple

Method

Dissolve Jell-o and gelatin in salt and boiling water.

Add all of Step Two to Step One blend well. Chill to thicken slightly. Whip until foamy with whisk.

Fold pineapple into foamy sour cream mixture.

Utensils

large bowl
measuring spoons
saucepan
measuring cup
whisk
can opener
large spoon

187

Cranberry - Tuna Mold

Ingredients

Step One

2 cans (13 oz.) tuna packed in water
1 cup mayonnaise

Step Two

1 can (8 oz.) sliced water chestnuts
2 Tablespoons frozen chopped onions
2 Tablespoons frozen chopped chives

Step Three

1 Tablespoon unflavored gelatin
1/4 cup cold water
1/4 cup boiling water

Method

Drain tuna. Put tuna in medium sized bowl and mash up with fork or wooden spoon. Mix mayonnaise and tuna well together.

Drain and roughly chop water chestnuts. Add thawed onions, chives and chopped water chestnuts to Step One.

Put gelatin into a small bowl, add cold water to soften. Pour boiling water into bowl to dissolve gelatin. Mix well. Scrape gelatin into tuna mixture and stir well. Put into 8" x 8" pan. Chill until firm.

Topping of Cranberry Tuna Mold

Ingredients

Method

Step One

1 (3 oz.) box of lemon gelatin
3/4 cup boiling water

Put gelatin in 2 qt. mixing bowl and pour boiling water over gelatin. Mix well.

Step Two

1/4 cup slivered almonds
1 can whole cranberry sauce
1/4 cup orange juice

Melt sauce just until liquid. Add almonds and juice to sauce. Mix into lemon gelatin. Spoon over chilled tuna base. Chill until firm.

Cut into squares. Serve on a bed of lettuce. Garnish with a dollop of creamy mayonnaise.* This salad should be made a day ahead.

*(Creamy mayonnaise is half mayonnaise and half sour cream.)

Shopping List

2 cans (13 oz.) light tuna packed in water
1 cup mayonnaise
1 8 oz. can sliced water chestnuts
2 Tablespoons frozen chopped onions
2 Tablespoons frozen chopped chives
1 Tablespoon unflavored gelatin
1 (3 oz.) box lemon gelatin
1/4 cup slivered almonds
1 can (16 oz.) whole cranberry sauce
1/4 cup orange juice

Utensils

can opener
2 medium sized bowls
1 small bowl
fork or wooden spoon
measuring cups
measuring spoons
knife to chop
chopping board
1 qt. saucepan or smaller
8" x 8" pan something equal in size

Notes

Marinated Shrimp Salad

Ingredients

Step One

1 cup cooked small
  Alaskan Bay shrimp
1/2 cup Italian salad dressing

Step Two

1 cup rice

Step Three

4 oz. carrots

1/4 cup diced celery

Step Four

1 cup frozen peas

Method

Marinate shrimp in dressing overnight.

Cook in plenty of water for 15 minutes.

While rice is cooking, grate carrots with food processor.
Dice in food processor and add carrots and celery to rice. Cook 2 minutes, then drain.
Put into large bowl.

Add to rice when drained.

Step Five

1/2 cup Italian dressing
1 Tablespoon dijon mustard
1 teaspoon salt
2 dashes Worcestershire sauce
1/2 cup sweet pickle relish, drained

Combine together and mix in with rice. Chill overnight.

Next Day

Step Six

1/4 cup chopped black olives
drained marinated shrimp

Mix olives and shrimp in with rice. Serve on a bed of lettuce garnished with tomatoes and whatever else strikes your fancy.

Shopping List

1 cup cooked canned, frozen or fresh
   small Alaskan Bay shrimp
8 oz. Italian salad dressing
1 cup uncooked rice
3-4 carrots
1 stalk of celery
1 cup frozen peas
dijon style mustard
salt
Worcestershire sauce
1/2 cup sweet pickle relish
1/4 cup chopped black olives

Utensils

1 pint bowl
measuring cup
2-3 qt. saucepan
food processor
knife
large bowl
collander
measuring spoons
large spoon
can opener

Seafood Salad with Herbs

Ingredients

Step One

1 # cooked torsk or lobster
8 oz. crabmeat
1½ dz. medium cooked shrimp

Step Two

1½ cups mayonnaise

Step Three

3/4 cup celery, diced
1/4 cup minced dry parsley
3 Tablespoons minced dried chives
2 teaspoons tarragon
pinch of dry mustard

Step Four

Method

Pick over crab. Leave seafood in small chunks. Do not flake. Drain moisture out of crab. Chill.

Put in mixing bowl.

Add all of Step Three to Step Two and mix well.

Mix Step One in with mayonnaise. Arrange on a bed of lettuce. Garnish with thin slices or wedges of tomatoes and quartered eggs, pimento, black olives and artichoke hearts (optional).

Shopping List

1 # torsk or lobster
8 oz. crabmeat
1½ dz. medium shrimp
1½ cups mayonnaise
3-4 stalks celery
1/4 cup minced dried chives
3 Tablespoons minced dried chives
tarragon
dry mustard
2 tomatoes
2-3 hard cooked eggs
1 head Boston lettuce
1 small jar whole pimentos
black olives
1 small can artichoke hearts, optional

Utensils

saucepan for eggs
2 mixing bowls
measuring cup
knife
measuring spoon
means to open jar
can opener
platter

Notes

Desserts

Desserts

Strawberry Mousse

Ingredients

Step One

1 cup strawberry puree

Step Two

1 Tablespoon gelatin, unflavored
2 Tablespoons boiling water

Step Three

2 cups whipping cream
1/2 cup sugar
2 Tablespoons plus triple sec

Step Four

Method

Cut strawberries in half and put through food processor. Then strain or cut up and cook in saucepan until liquid and can be put through a strainer.

Soften gelatin in hot water. Slowly add a small amount of puree to gelatin. Then pour the gelatin mixture into the cup of puree.

With an electric mixer, whip cream. Gradually add sugar and triple sec. Keep beating until soft peaks are formed. Do not overbeat.

Gradually fold strawberry puree into whipped cream mixture. Refrigerate.

Shopping List

1 # bag frozen strawberries
1 pkg. unflavored gelatin
2 cups whipping cream
1/2 cup sugar
2 Tablespoons triple sec

Utensils

measuring cup
measuring spoon
mixing bowl
food processor, optional
strainer
small saucepan
mixer, hand or stationary
knife

Notes

Coffee Mousse

Ingredients

Step One

1 Tablespoon unflavored gelatin
1/4 cup coffee liqueur

Step Two

1/2 cup strong HOT coffee

Step Three

1/4 cup coffee liqueur
2/3 cup sugar

Step Four

1½ cup whipping cream

Optional: May be garnished with chocolate shavings. May be served in chocolate cups with shavings. Fills 10 cups.

Method

In a 2 qt. mixing bowl, soften gelatin in coffee liqueur.

Pour into Step One and dissolve gelatin.

Mix into Step Two when gelatin is dissolved.

Beat until soft peaks form, then fold into above. Chill in serving container or sherbets.

Shopping List

1 pkg. unflavored gelatin
1/2 cup coffee
1/2 cup coffee liqueur
2/3 cup sugar
1½ whipping cream
chocolate cups, optional
semi-sweet chocolate, optional

Utensils

2 qt. mixing bowl
measuring spoons
measuring cup
electric mixer or power whisk
spoon
grater, optional
serving bowl or individual bowls

Notes

Poached Pears

Ingredients

Step One

6 pears (fresh)

Step Two

2 cups port
1/2 cup water
1/2 cup sugar
1 stick cinnamon

Step Three

Method

Peel pears but leave stem on.

Mix ingredients of Step Two together in a saucepan large enough to hold pears upright.

Simmer pears 20 minutes. Cool pears down in the liquid. Chill in liquid. Refrigerate covered overnight. Serve pears with their liquid.

Shopping List

6 pears
2 cups port
1/2 cup sugar
1 stick cinnamon

Utensils

peeler
saucepan large enough
 to hold pears upright
serving dish for pears
measuring cup

Drake Bananas

Ingredients

Step One

2 bananas, mashed
2 cups water
1/2 cup sugar
1/2 tsp. cinnamon

Step Two

6 bananas sliced in thirds

Step Three

1/4 cup triple sec, optional

Shopping List

8 bananas
1/2 cup sugar
cinnamon
triple sec, optional

Method

Step One

Combine together and simmer in 4 qt. saucepan for 20 minutes.

Step Two

Add these bananas to cooking liquid of Step One. Simmer 10 minutes. Remove from liquid with slotted spoon and cool.

Step Three

Continue cooking liquid until reduced by half. When ready to serve - spoon a little liquid over bananas.

Utensils

measuring cup
measuring spoons
knife
4 qt. saucepan
slotted spoon
bowl for the bananas

Fruit Ambrosia

Ingredients

Step One

1 can (8 oz.) mandarin orange sections
1 can (8 oz.) grapefruit sections
1/4 cup coconut
1/4 cup Kirsch

Method

Drain fruit and combine. Add kirsch to the fruit and mix in bowl. Sprinkle with coconut before serving.

Shopping List

1 can (8 oz.) mandarin orange sections
1 can (8 oz.) grapefruit sections
1/4 cup kirsch
1/4 cup coconut

Utensils

can opener
strainer
measuring cup
scissors
bowl

Notes

Melon Pears

Ingredients

Step One

1/2 cup sugar
1 quart water
1/2 cup midori liqueur

Step Two

6 bartlett pears

Step Three

Shopping List

6 bartlett pears
1/2 cup sugar
1/2 cup midori liquor

Method

In a large saucepan in which the pears will fit. Poach the syrup for 10 minutes and stir.

Peel pears leaving on stem. Set pears in saucepan and poach pears 30 minutes.

Remove pears with a slotted spoon. Chill. Reduce liquid until it is about 1½ cups. When ready to serve, spoon a little liquid over pears.

Utensils

large saucepan
measuring cup
peeler
slotted spoon
bowl for pears

Chocolate Sauce

Ingredients

Step One

8 squares, unsweetened chocolate
8 oz. butter

Step Two

3½ cups confectioners sugar
10 oz. evaporated milk

May be made ahead. May be refrigerated and then reheated. Keeps well for several weeks.

Shopping List

8 squares unsweetened chocolate
8 oz. butter
3½ cups confectioners sugar
10 oz. evaporated milk

Method

Melt in the top of a double boiler over moderate heat.

Add Step Two ingredients to Step One. Stir over moderate heat until well blended.

Utensils

double boiler
spoon
measuring cup
pointed can opener
storage jar

Raspberry Sauce

Ingredients

Step One

1 frozen pouch of raspberries

Step Two

1/4 cup kirsch or triple sec

Shopping List

1 frozen pouch of raspberries
1/4 cup kirsch or triple sec

Method

Thaw completely. Put raspberries in a strainer over a saucepan. Rub through strainer gently with a spoon. Throw away the seeds. Simmer the raspberries, reducing a small amount.

Add liqueur to the sauce, simmer 1-2 minutes.

Use this sauce for berries or poached fruit.

Utensils

strainer
spoon
scissors
saucepan
measuring cup

Chocolate Velvet

Ingredients

Method

Step One

5 egg yolks
1/3 cup sugar

Beat with mixer until light and lemon colored.

Step Two

1 cup evaporated milk
4 oz. semi-sweet chocolate morsels

Heat milk in saucepan and add morsels. Stir until blended and smooth.

Step Three

1 Tablespoon gelatin
2 Tablespoons triple sec

Fold Step One into Step Two. Cool. Soften gelatin in triple sec, then add to chocolate mixture.

Step Four

1 cup heavy cream

Whip cream until soft firm peaks form. Fold into chocolate mixture. Put into individual serving dishes or a 4 qt. bowl. Refrigerate until set.

Shopping List

5 eggs
1/3 cup sugar
1 cup evaporated milk
4 oz. semi-sweet chocolate morsels
1 Tablespoon gelatin
2 Tablespoons triple sec
1 cup heavy cream

Utensils

electric mixer and bowl
measuring cup
pointed can opener
small bowl
saucepan
wooden spoon or whisk
serving dish
measuring cup

Notes

Pecan Cookies

Ingredients

Step One

4 oz. butter
1/2 cup brown sugar

Step Two

1/2 cup molasses

Step Three

1/2 cup flour
1 teaspoon baking powder

Step Four

1 egg, beaten
1 cup chopped pecans

Method

Cream together. This can be done by hand or better in a food processor.

Mix into Step One.

Combine well with Step One.

Mix well with Step One. Drop by 1/2 teaspoon on greased baking sheet 2" apart. Bake at 350° for 10-12 minutes or until done.

Shopping List

4 oz. butter
1/2 cup brown sugar
1/2 cup molasses
1/2 cup flour
1 teaspoon baking powder
1 egg
1 cup chopped pecans
shortening (a dab)

Utensils

food processor, very helpful
   or
mixer and bowl
measuring cup
measuring spoons
baking sheet

Notes

Date Squares

Ingredients

Step One

1 cup sugar
1 teaspoon vanilla
3 eggs

Step Two

1 teaspoon baking powder
1½ cups sifted flour

Step Three

1 cup chopped walnuts
1½ cups chopped dates
flour

Step Four

Method

Beat until light and fluffy.

Mix dates with a little flour. Add walnuts and dates to flour and egg mixture. Combine Steps One, Two and Three.

Put in a 9" x 9" pan and bake at 325° for 40 minutes or until done. Cut into bars and dust with powdered sugar.

Shopping List

3 eggs
1 cup sugar
1 teaspoon vanilla
baking powder
1¾ cup flour
1 cup chopped walnuts
1 pkg. dates
powdered sugar

Utensils

food processor or
knife
scissors
measuring cup
measuring spoons
sifter or strainer
9" x 9" baking pan
spoon

Notes

Chocolate Chip Bars

Ingredients

Step One

1 egg
12 oz. yellow cake mix
1/2 cup melted butter

Method

Beat egg lightly in bowl large enough to hold ingredients of Step One. Add cake mix and melted butter. Beat until smooth. Pour into 9" x 13" baking pan, pat smooth and bake at 350° for 12 -15 minutes. Cool.

Step Two

3 eggs
1½ cups brown sugar
1/4 cup yellow cake mix
1½ teaspoon vanilla
2 cups coconut
1½ cups chocolate chips (9 oz.)

In unwashed bowl from above, beat eggs well. Gradually add brown sugar, cake mix, vanilla, coconut and chocolate chips. Smooth over cooled cake bottom and bake at 350° for 30 - 35 minutes. When cool, cut into bars either 2" x 2" or 1" x 2".

Hint: An easy way to cut the bars is to cool completely to room temperature. Then cut around the outside of the pan. Put a cookie sheet on top of the pan and flip the pan over. Give the bottom of the baking pan a thump or two and remove pan. Then proceed upon your way to cut the bars.

As the corners are rounded, I always use that as an excuse to taste this warm from the oven.

Shopping List

4 eggs
16 oz. yellow cake mix
4 oz. butter
1½ cups brown sugar
1½ teaspoon vanilla
2 cups coconut
9 oz. chocolate chips

Utensils

large mixing bowl
electric mixer
saucepan to melt butter
9" x 13" baking pan
spatula
measuring cup
measuring spoons knife
tin to store bars in

Notes

Sauces, Dips and Marinades

Sauces, Dips and Marinades

Anchovy Sauce

To basic white sauce for fish
ADD

Ingredients

3 Tablespoons anchovy paste
1 Tablespoon butter, softened
1 Tablespoon lemon juice

Method

Mix together and add to sauce.

Utensils

measuring spoon
wooden spoon
knife to cut lemon

Notes

Cheese Sauce

To basic white sauce for fish
ADD

Ingredients

1/2 cup grated mozzarella
1/4 cup grated parmesan
1/4 cup sherry

Method

Stir into hot sauce.

Utensils

measuring cup
whisk

Notes

GINGER SNAPS

(A crisp, crunchy cooky)

Yield: 10 dozen small cookies

¾ cup Swift'ning Shortening
¾ cup brown sugar, packed
1 egg
¾ cup molasses
3 cups sifted flour

¼ teaspoon salt
2 teaspoons soda
½ teaspoon cloves
1 teaspoon cinnamon
1 teaspoon ginger

Cream Swift'ning. Add sugar gradually and continue creaming. Add egg and molasses. Beat well. Sift flour with salt, soda, and spices. Mix well. Chill in refrigerator. (This dough is soft and must be thoroughly chilled in order to shape.) Form into small balls. Roll in sugar. Place 2 inches apart on cooky sheet. Bake in moderate oven (375° F.) about 10 minutes. Store in loosely covered container to retain crispness.

PEANUT OATMEAL DROPS

(A crisp drop cooky)

Yield: 6 dozen 3-inch cookies

1 cup Swift'ning Shortening
1 cup granulated sugar
1 cup brown sugar, packed
1 teaspoon vanilla

2 eggs
1½ cups sifted flour
1 teaspoon soda
3 cups rolled oats

½ pound salted Spanish peanuts

Cream Swift'ning; add sugars gradually. Add vanilla and continue creaming. Add eggs and beat well. Sift flour with soda and add. Stir in rolled oats and peanuts and blend thoroughly. Form dough with hands into small balls. Place on cooky sheet and flatten slightly. Bake in hot oven (425° F.) about 7 minutes. Store in tightly covered container to retain crispness.

SOFT MOLASSES COOKIES

(A soft cake-like cooky)

Yield: 10 dozen

¾ cup Swift'ning Shortening
1 cup sugar
2 eggs
1 cup molasses
4 cups sifted flour

1 teaspoon salt
1 teaspoon soda
2 teaspoons cinnamon
2 teaspoons ginger
¾ cup water

Cream Swift'ning and sugar together. Add the eggs. Mix well. Add the molasses. Sift flour, salt, soda, and spices together and add alternately with water. Drop by teaspoonfuls (size of walnut) on cooky sheet. Bake in moderate oven (375° F.) about 12 minutes. Cookies will spread just slightly during baking. Keep in covered tin to assure cookies' retaining their softness. Cookies are 2 inches in diameter after baking.

PEANUT BUTTER CRUNCHIES

(A crisp cooky)

Yield: 4 to 5 dozen small cookies

½ cup Swift'ning Shortening
½ cup peanut butter
½ cup brown sugar, packed
½ cup granulated sugar

½ teaspoon vanilla
1 egg
1½ cups sifted flour
1 teaspoon soda

1 teaspoon salt

Cream Swift'ning and peanut butter. Add sugars and vanilla and mix until fluffy. Add egg and beat well. Sift together dry ingredients and blend into sugar mixture. Shape into small balls. Place on cooky sheet 2 inches apart. Flatten with tines of fork dipped in sugar. Bake in a moderate oven (375° F.) about 10 minutes. Store in loosely covered container.

PECAN TEA COOKIES

(A rich crisp cooky)

Yield: About 6 dozen

1 cup Swift'ning Shortening	2 cups sifted flour
½ cup sugar	½ teaspoon salt
2 teaspoons vanilla	2 cups finely chopped pecans
	Powdered sugar

Cream Swift'ning, sugar, and vanilla until fluffy. Sift flour with salt and add to creamed mixture, blending thoroughly. Add pecans, mix well. Shape into 1-inch balls and place on cooky sheet. Bake in a slow oven (325° F.) about 20 minutes. *Do not brown.* Cool, then roll in powdered sugar. Store in loosely covered container to assure cookies' retaining their crispness.

Cocoa Nut Balls: Add ¼ cup cocoa to recipe for Pecan Tea Cookies. Bake as directed.

REFRIGERATOR COOKIES

(A crisp cooky)

Yield: 8 dozen small cookies

1 cup Swift'ning Shortening	3½ cups sifted flour
2 cups brown sugar, packed	1 teaspoon salt
2 teaspoons vanilla	1 teaspoon soda
2 eggs	1 cup finely chopped nuts

Cream Swift'ning, brown sugar, and vanilla. Add eggs and mix well. Sift together flour, salt, and soda. Add nuts and combine with creamed mixture. Mold into 2 rolls (2 inches in diameter), wrap in waxed paper, and put into refrigerator over night or until needed. Chill rolls ½ hour in freezing compartment of refrigerator for ease in cutting cookies. Slice very thin, bake on cooky sheet in a moderate oven (375° F.) about 8 minutes. Store in loosely covered cooky jar to assure cookies' remaining crisp.

BROWNIES

(A chewy chocolate bar)

Yield: 7x11-inch pan

⅓ cup Swift'ning Shortening	1 cup sugar
¾ cup sifted flour	2 eggs
½ teaspoon double-acting baking powder	½ teaspoon vanilla
½ teaspoon salt	2—1-ounce squares unsweetened
1 cup chopped pecans	chocolate, melted

Sift together flour, baking powder, and salt; stir in pecans. Cream Swift'ning and gradually beat in sugar. Add eggs, vanilla, and chocolate; stir in flour-pecan mixture. Turn into 7x11-inch pan (rubbed with Swift'ning) and bake in a moderate oven (350° F.) 22 minutes. *Do not overbake.* Cut into 24 squares. Keep covered. Brownies are best when fresh.

COCONUT DROP COOKIES

(A crisp cooky)

Yield: 60—1-inch cookies

1 cup Swift'ning Shortening	1 teaspoon soda
1 cup granulated sugar	1 teaspoon baking powder
1 cup brown sugar, packed	½ teaspoon salt
2 eggs	1 teaspoon vanilla
2 cups sifted flour	2 cups rolled oats
	2 cups shredded coconut

Cream the Swift'ning and sugars until light and fluffy. Add the eggs and beat well. Sift flour, soda, baking powder, and salt, and add to creamed mixture. Add vanilla. Stir in rolled oats and coconut. Drop by teaspoonful on cooky sheet. Bake in a moderate oven (350° F.) about 12 minutes or until light golden brown. Store in loosely covered container to assure cookies' retaining their crispness.

Basic White Sauce for Fish

Ingredients

Step One

4 Tablespoons butter
3 Tablespoons flour

Step Two

1/2 cup clam juice

Step Three

1/2 cup half & half
1/2 cup homogenized milk

Step Four

salt and pepper

Method

Step One

Melt butter in skillet. Add the flour and stir constantly until slightly colored. Do not burn.

Step Two

Off heat, stir in half of clam juice whisking. Return to heat and add the rest of the clam juice whisking to get rid of the lumps.

Step Three

Gradually stir Step Three into Step Two. Continue simmering until thickened.

Step Four

Season to taste.

Shopping List

2 oz. butter
3 Tablespoons flour
4 oz. clam juice
4 oz. half & half
4 oz. homogenized milk

Utensils

skillet
whisk
bottle or can opener
measuring cup
measuring spoon

Notes

Basic Sauce Veloute

Ingredients

Step One

2 Tablespoons flour
2 Tablespoons butter

Step Two

1¼ cups stock
salt and pepper

Method

Melt butter in skillet. Add the flour and stir constantly until slightly colored. Do not burn.

Off heat, stir in half of stock with whisk. Return to heat and mix in rest of stock. Whisking to get rid of any lumps. Simmer 10-12 minutes and add salt and pepper to tast.
This is a base for sauces only.

Utensils

measuring spoon
measuring cup
whisk
skillet

Oyster Sauce

Ingredients

Step One

2 Tablespoons flour
2 Tablespoons butter

Step Two

3/4 cup clam juice
1/4 cup oyster liquor
1/4 cup sherry

Step Three

1/2 cup fresh or frozen oysters

Shopping List

flour
2 Tablespoons butter
6 oz. clam juice
1/2 cup oysters with their liquor
1/4 cup sherry

Method

Melt butter in skillet. Add the flour and stir constantly until slightly colored. Do not burn.

Combine Step Two in a bowl. Off heat, stir in half of Step Two into Step One. Return to heat and mix in rest of liquid whisking to get rid of any lumps. Simmer 10 minutes.

Add oysters to Step Two and continue cooking until edges of oysters curl.

Utensils

skillet
whisk
means to open clam juice
measuring cup
measuring spoon
knife

Shrimp Sauce

Ingredients

Step One

2 Tablespoons flour
2 Tablespoons butter

Step Two

1 cup clam juice

Step Three

1/2 cup frozen baby shrimp, drained
1/4 cup dry vermouth

Shopping List

flour
butter
8 oz. clam juice
4 oz. baby shrimp
1/4 cup dry vermouth

Method

Melt butter in skillet. Add the flour and stir constantly until slightly colored. Do not burn.

Off heat, stir in half of clam juice. Return to heat and mix in rest of clam juice. Whisk to get rid of lumps. Simmer 10-12 minutes and add salt and pepper to taste.

Stir into hot sauce.

Utensils

measuring spoons
measuring cup
skillet
scissors
means to open bottles

Hot New Orleans Remoulade for Shrimp

Ingredients

1/4 cup horseradish
1/2 cup hot mustard
1/4 teaspoon garlic powder
1½ cups frozen diced onions
1/4 teaspoons celery seed
2 Tablespoons paprika
2 teaspoons freeze dried parsley flakes
3/4 cup olive oil
1/4 cup salad oil
2 Tablespoons Worcestershire sauce
1/4 teaspoon Tabasco

Utensils

measuring cup
measuring spoon
whisk or spoon
1-2 qt. bowl

Dill Sauce 2

Ingredients

1/2 cup dijon style mustard
1/4 cup fresh or frozen lemon juice
1 cup mayonnaise, NOT salad dressing
2 Tablespoons sugar
1/4 cup white wine vinegar
4 Tablespoons dried dill weed
2 Tablespoons dried parsley

Method

Dissolve sugar in vinegar and then add all other ingredients and mix well. Make ahead for maximum flavor, then refrigerate.

Utensils

measuring cup
measuring spoon
1 qt. bowl
whisk

Notes

Almond Sauce for Fish

Ingredients

Step One

4 oz. butter
3/4 cup slivered almonds

Step Two

1/8 teaspoon garlic powder
2 Tablespoons dry vermouth
1/8 teaspoon white pepper
1/2 teaspoon salt or to taste

Shopping List

4 oz. butter
6 oz. slivered almonds
garlic powder
2 Tablespoons dry vermouth
salt
white pepper

Method

Melt butter in skillet. Cook almonds over low heat until they are brown.

Add all of Step Two to Step One. Pour over sautéed fish.

Utensils

skillet
wooden spoon
measuring spoons
measuring cup

Herb Seasoned Mayonnaise

For cold fish or shellfish

Ingredients

1½ cups mayonnaise
1/4 teaspoon dried chives
1/4 teaspoon dried parsley
1/8 teaspoon garlic powder
1/2 teaspoon dried tarragon

Make ahead for full flavor

Utensils

measuring cup
measuring spoons
whisk
1 qt. bowl

Sauce Verte

Ingredients

2 Tablespoons dried parsley
1/2 cup frozen chopped spinach,
  drained well
1 Tablespoon dried chives
1 teaspoon Beau Monde seasoning
1 cup mayonnaise
1 cup sour cream

Method

Mix together.
Serve with cold fish or shell fish.

Utensils

measuring cup
measuring spoon
spoon or whisk
1 qt. bowl

Notes

Herb Butter

For fish or to add to sauce for fish

Ingredients

3 teaspoons dried parsley
2 teaspoons chervil
2 teaspoons chives
1 teaspoons tarragon
4 oz. softened butter
salt
white pepper

Method

Mix together, all ingredients. Store sealed in refrigerator. A dab of herb butter jazzes up a fish fillet.

Utensils

measuring spoons
wooden spoon
bowl
container to store butter

Notes

Creole Barbecue

Ingredients

Step One

4 oz. butter

Step Two

1½ cups frozen chopped onions
1/4 teaspoon garlic powder
1/2 cup frozen chopped green peppers
1 rib celery, sliced

Step Three

2 cans (16 oz.) peeled Italian tomatoes
1 can (8 oz.) tomato puree
1/2 cup sweet vermouth
1/2 cup brown sugar
2 Tablespoons vinegar
1 teaspoon salt
1 teaspoon pepper
dash Tabasco

Method

Melt in saucepan.

Sauté all of Step Two in butter.

Add all of Step Three to Step Two.
Simmer 30 minutes uncovered.

Shopping List

4 oz. butter
1½ cups frozen chopped onions
1/4 teaspoon garlic powder
1/2 cup frozen chopped green peppers
1 celery rib
2 cans (16 oz.) peeled Italian tomatoes
1 (8 oz.) tomato puree
1/2 cup sweet vermouth
1/2 cup brown sugar
2 Tablespoons vinegar
Tabasco
salt and pepper

Utensils

saucepan
can opener
measuring spoon
measuring cup
knife
spoon

Notes

Red Wine Marinade for Beef

Ingredients

2 cups beaujolais wine
1/3 cup brandy
1/4 cup olive oil
1/2 cup sliced carrots
1 cup frozen diced onions
1/2 cup sliced celery
2 garlic cloves, unpeeled and
   cut in half
1½ teaspoons thyme
1 bay leaf
2 whole cloves
1½ teaspoons salt

Method

Marinate 24 hours in refrigerator.

Reserve marinade. Reduce over moderate heat to half the amount. Baste meat with this juice. Strain and serve with meat.

Utensils

measuring cup
measuring spoons
knife
3 qt. container to mix marinade

Ham Marinade

Ingredients

1/2 cup honey
1/4 cup vinegar
1 teaspoon dry mustard
1/8 teaspoon garlic powder
1/4 cup vermouth
6 oz. pineapple juice

Method

Heat through and simmer 2 minutes.
Add 6 oz. pineapple juice.

Utensils

measuring cup
measuring spoon
can opener

Notes

Marinade for Spareribs

Ingredients

1/2 cup soy sauce
1/2 cup water
1/2 cup red wine
1 Tablespoon honey
1 teaspoon salt
1/8 teaspoon garlic powder

Utensils

measuring cup
measuring spoon
1 qt. container

Notes

Lemon Marinade for Poultry

Marinate 6 hours in refrigerator

Ingredients

1/2 cup lemon juice
1/4 cup peanut oil
2 Tablespoons minced dry onions
1/8 teaspoon garlic powder
1/2 teaspoon Beau Monde seasoning
1/2 teaspoon pepper

Method

Baste poultry with marinade while cooking.

Utensils

measuring cup
measuring spoon
1-2 qt. container

Notes

Lime Marinade for Poultry

Ingredients

1/2 cup peanut oil
1/2 cup lime juice
2 Tablespoons dry minced onions
2 teaspoons rubbed tarragon
1/2 teaspoon Tabasco
1 teaspoon Worcestershire sauce

Marinate 6 hours in
refrigerator
Baste poultry with
marinade.

Utensils

measuring cup
measuring spoon
1-2 qt. container

236

Tomato Sauce for Meats

Ingredients

Step One

1/4 cup grated carrots
1/2 cup chopped frozen onions
1/4 teaspoon ground celery seed
2 Tablespoons real bacon bits
3 Tablespoons butter
1 Tablespoon oil

Step Two

1½ Tablespoons flour

Step Three

1½ cups simmering beef stock
    or broth

Method

Grate in food processor. Cook vegetables and bacon slowly in butter and oil for 10 minutes.

Blend flour into Step One. Continue cooking 3-5 minutes more.

Take vegetable flour mixture off heat and mix in stock.

Step Four

1½ cups tomato puree
1½ cups water
1/4 teaspoon salt
1 cup sweet vermouth
2 unpeeled cloves garlic
1 teaspoon dried minced parsley
1/2 bay leaf
1/4 teaspoon thyme

Combine all of Step Four with vegetables. Simmer 1½ hours. Add water if it gets too thick.

Step Five

Strain juices, pressing through a strainer. This sauce may be frozen.

Shopping List

1 carrot
1/2 cup frozen chopped onions
ground celery seed
2 Tablespoons real bacon bits
3 Tablespoons butter
oil
flour
1½ cups beef broth or stock
1½ cups tomato puree
salt
1/4 cup sweet vermouth
2 cloves garlic
dry minced parsley
bay leaf
thyme

Utensils

food processor
2 qt. saucepan
wooden spoon
measuring cup
measuring spoons
knife
strainer

Curry Cream Dip for Fresh Vegetables

Ingredients

Step One

1/4-1/2 teaspoon curry powder
1 Tablespoon oil

Step Two

1 cup mayonnaise
1/2 cup sour cream
1 Tablespoon minced dill weed
1 teaspoon Worcestershire sauce
1/4 teaspoon salt
1 Tablespoon minced dry onion
1½ teaspoon lemon juice
1 teaspoon capers, drained and minced

Serve with fresh vegetables

Method

Heat oil and curry in skillet for 1-2 minutes being careful not to scorch.

Mix together in bowl. Add heated curry. Stir well.

Utensils

measuring spoons
measuring cup
small skillet
1 qt. bowl

Dill Dip

Ingredients

Step One

1 cup mayonnaise
1 cup sour cream
1 Tablespoon dill weed
1 Tablespoon parsley flakes
1 teaspoon Beau Monde seasoning
1 Tablespoon minced dry onion
1/8 teaspoon garlic powder
3-4 drops Tabasco sauce

This dip makes an excellent dip for fresh vegetables.

Method

Mix all ingredients together. Store in sealed container in refrigerator.

Shopping List

1 cup mayonnaise
1 cup sour cream
dill weed
parsley flakes
Beau Monde seasoning
minced dry onions
garlic powder
Tabasco

Utensils

measuring spoon
bowl
measuring cup
whisk or spoon
container for dip

Cucumber Sauce

Ingredients

Step One

1 cup cucumber

Step Two

1/2 cup mayonnaise
1/2 cup sour cream
2 teaspoons dill
1/2 teaspoon salt
1/8 teaspoon pepper

Shopping List

2 cucumbers
1/2 cup mayonnaise
1/2 cup sour cream
dill
salt
pepper

Method

Peel and coarsely chop by hand or with a food processor. Salt, let drain in strainer. Pat dry on paper towels.

Mix well in bowl and then add Step One to Step Two.

Utensils

food processor, optional
vegetable peeler
knife
measuring spoon
measuring cup
mixing bowl
rubber spatula

Cucumber Cream Dressing

Ingredients

Step One

1 cucumber

Step Two

1/3 cup heavy cream
1 cup mayonnaise

Step Three

1/2 teaspoon salt
2 teaspoon dry minced onion
2 teaspoon dry minced parsley

Step Four

Method

Peel and chop. Sprinkle with salt, drain in collander then paper towel.

Whip cream, then fold into mayonnaise.

Mix into Step Two.

Mix cucumber into Step Two. Refrigerate.

Excellent for salmon.

Shopping List

1 cucumber
1/3 cup heavy cream
1 cup mayonnaise
salt
dry minced onion
dry minced parsley

Utensils

peeler
knife
measuring cup
measuring spoon
1 qt. container, bowl
spoon
collander
paper towel

Notes

Spinach Salad Dressing

Ingredients

Step One

1/2 cup sugar
1 teaspoon salt
1 Tablespoon cornstarch

Step Two

2 well beaten eggs

Step Three

3/4 cup cider vinegar

To serve

Mix with equal parts mayonnaise,
  NOT salad dressing.

Method

Put in top of double boiler and mix together.

Add to Step One and mix well.

Gradually add to Step Two and cook in double boiler until thick. Store in refrigerator.

Utensils

measuring cup
measuring spoon
whisk
1 qt. bowl
double boiler
jar for storage

Honey Dressing for Fruit Salad

Ingredients

Step One

1/3 cup superfine sugar
1/3 cup white wine vinegar

Step Two

1 teaspoon Hungarian sweet paprika
1 teaspoon dry mustard
1 teaspoon celery seed
1 teaspoon light salt
1 Tablespoon lemon juice
dash of onion powder
1/3 cup honey

Step Three

1 cup corn oil

Method

Blender or food processor. Put sugar in processor. Pour vinegar over sugar and let stand 3-5 minutes. Whirl in processor a few times to dissolve.

Put all ingredients of Step Two into processor and whirl several times.

Slowly add corn oil to ingredients in processor while processor is going. Pour into jar with lid. Refrigerate. Makes about 2 cups.

Shopping List

1/3 cup superfine sugar
1/3 cup honey
1/3 cup white wine vinegar
Hungarian sweet paprika
dry mustard
light salt
celery seed
lemon juice
1 cup corn oil

Utensils

measuring cup
measuring spoons
food processor
   or
electric blender
spatula
pint jar with tight fitting lid

Notes

Quiches - Miscellaneous

Quiches

Quiches

The classsic quiche is made in a quiche pan, normally either ovenproof china or metal. This requires making and rolling out the dough. If you are able to roll out the dough, by all means do so with your favorite one crust recipe. However, if you cannot roll out the dough, do not let this stop you from enjoying this delicious treat. There are quite a number of good prepared pie crusts on the market.

Although the recipes call for whipping cream, you can certainly substitute half and half. Granted, when you substitute the quiche will not be quite the same. However, it will still be tasty.

One easy way of mixing the quiche batter is to put it in a jar with a lid so that you can shake it provided your grip is good enough to hold onto the jar. Then, you can pour directly from the jar into the pie shell. Another method is to mix the batter in a mixing bowl with a handle such as the one pictured in this book.

If possible, you might have someone with a food processor grate several pounds of cheese. Then you can freeze it in various amounts depending upon what is called for in most of your recipes.

I have found it easier to cut the quiche before reheating it. Quiche can be frozen. However, it will not be quite as good as when it has been just refrigerated.

Quiche is a very flexible dish. It can be served for brunch, lunch, supper, cocktail appetizers, and late night suppers. It goes happily with cut fruits, fruit salads, stuffed large mushrooms, and many other foods.

Try it and enjoy it.

Spinach Quiche

Ingredients

Step One

10 oz. frozen chopped spinach
9" prepared pie shell

Step Two

2 Tablespoons butter
3 Tablespoons diced frozen onions
3 oz. grated parmesan cheese

Step Three

4 eggs lightly beaten
1½ cups whipping cream
1/2 teaspoon salt
1/4 teaspoon white pepper
1/4 teaspoon nutmeg

Method

Thaw and drain in strainer by gently pushing spinach into strainer.

Thaw onions and saute in butter. Cook until translucent. Add spinach to onions and cook until dry. Mix in cheese and spread on bottom of pie shell.

Mix all of Step Three ingredients together. Pull oven rack part way out of oven. Put pie shell on rack. Pour egg/cream mixture into shell over the spinach.

Step Four

3 oz. grated parmesan cheese

Quiche may be made ahead and refrigerated. Bring up to room temperature and then heat at 325° until heated through, approximately 20 minutes.

Sprinkle cheese on top of quiche. Push rack back into oven. Bake at 450° for 10 minutes. Turn oven down to 375° and continue baking for 30 minutes or until well set.

Shopping List

9" prepared pie shell
10 oz. package frozen
chopped spinach
3 Tablespoons frozen chopped onions
6 oz. grated parmesan cheese
4 eggs
1½ cups whipping cream
salt
white pepper
nutmeg

Utensils

strainer
knife to cut butter
skillet
bowl or jar to mix batter
measuring spoon
measuring cups

Notes

Mushroom Quiche

Ingredients

Step One

9" prepared pie shell
1/2 # mushrooms
2 Tablespoons butter

Step Two

3/4 cup grated swiss cheese

Step Three

4 eggs lightly beaten
2 cups whipping cream
1/2 teaspoon salt
1/4 teaspoon white pepper

Method

Food Processor advised. Clean, then dice mushrooms in food processor. Melt butter in skillet. Sauté mushrooms until they have released all their liquid and moisture has evaporated. Put mushrooms in bottom of pie shell.

Grate cheese in processor without having washed bowl after mushrooms were diced. Distribute cheese over mushrooms.

Beat cream, salt, and pepper in with eggs.

Step Four

Hint: Quiche may be made ahead and refrigerated. Bring quiche to room temperature, then reheat at 325° for 20 minutes or until heated through.

Pull oven rack part way out. Set quiche shell on rack. Pour cream mixture over cheese and mushrooms. Push rack back into oven. Bake at 450° for 10 minutes, turn down oven to 375° and continue baking for 30 minutes or until quiche is set.

Shopping List

9" prepared pie shell
1/2 # mushrooms
3 oz. swiss cheese
4 eggs
2 cups (1 pint) whipping cream
2 Tablespoons butter

Utensils

food processor
skillet
mixing bowl
whisk or fork
measuring spoon
measuring cup

Notes

Shrimp Quiche

Ingredients

Method

Step One

9" prepared pie shell
2 Tablespoons minced frozen chives
2 Tablespoons butter

Melt butter and cook chives briefly in small pan. Set aside.

Step Two

1 can (7½ oz.) shrimp or 4 oz. fresh shrimp, peeled and deveined

Drain the canned shrimp well. If using fresh shrimp - cook peeled shrimp with chive butter until shrimp turns pink. Chop shrimp into small pieces by hand or with processor. Pour chive butter over shrimp and put shrimp in bottom of pie shell.

Step Three

4 eggs
2 cups heavy cream
1/2 teaspoon salt
1/4 teaspoon white pepper
2 Tablespoons sherry
1 Tablespoon tomato paste

Beat eggs lightly in quart jar with lid or in bowl with handle. Add all other ingredients of Step Three to eggs and shake or mix.

Pull oven rack part way out. Set quiche shell on oven rack. Pour quiche batter into shell.

Step Four

1/4 cup parmesan cheese

Sprinkle on top of quiche. Push rack in. Bake at 450° for 10 minutes. Turn oven down to 375° and continue to bake for 30 minutes or until well set.

Shopping List

2 Tablespoons frozen minced chives
2 Tablespoons butter
1 can (7½ oz.) shrimp or
  4 oz. cooked and deveined shrimp
4 eggs
2 cups heavy cream
salt and pepper
2 Tablespoons (1 oz.) sherry
1 Tablespoon tomato paste
1/4 cup parmesan cheese
9" prepared pie shell

Utensils

measuring spoon
bowl or jar with lid
small pan
strainer
knife, if fresh shrimp used
measuring cup

Notes

Salmon Quiche

Ingredients

Step One

2 Tablespoons frozen chopped chives
3 Tablespoons butter
1 teaspoon dry dill weed

Step Two

5 oz. cooked or canned salmon

Step Three

4 eggs, lightly beaten
2 cups whipping cream
1/2 teaspoon salt
1/4 teaspoon white pepper
2 Tablespoons sherry

Step Four

1/4 cup grated parmesan cheese

Method

Cook in melted butter 1 minute.

Remove skin and bones from salmon. Flake with fingers or fork. Add to Step One. Put in bottom of pie shell.

Mix all ingredients of Step Three together. Pull oven rack part way out. Pour quiche batter into shell over salmon.

Sprinkle cheese on top of quiche. Push rack in. Bake at 450° for 10 minutes, turn oven down to 375° and continue to bake for 30 minutes or until well set.

Shopping List

9" prepared pie shell
frozen chopped chives
3 Tablespoons butter
dried dill weed
5 oz. cooked or canned salmon
4 eggs
2 cups whipping cream
salt
white pepper
2 Tablespoons sherry
1/4 cup grated parmesan

Utensils

saucepan or skillet
bowl or jar for quiche batter
whisk or fork
measuring spoons
measuring cup
can opener, if canned salmon is used

Notes

Sausage Quiche

Ingredients

Method

Step One

9" prepared pie shell
1/2 # precooked sausage patties,
  thawed

Crumble and put in bottom of pie shell.

Step Two

3/4 cup grated Swiss cheese

Grate cheese and sprinkle over sausage.

Step Three

2 cups whipping cream
1/2 teaspoon salt
1/4 teaspoon white pepper
1/4 teaspoon nutmeg
4 eggs, lightly beaten

Mix all ingredients of Step Three in a bowl. Pull rack part way out of oven. Put quiche shell on rack. Pour slowly egg/cream mixture over sausage and cheese.

Step Four

1/4 cup grated parmesan cheese

Sprinkle over top of quiche. Push rack bake in oven.

Bake at 450° for 10 minutes, then turn down oven to 375° for 30 minutes or until set.

Shopping List

9" prepared pie shell
3 oz. Swiss cheese
1/2 # precooked sausage
salt
white pepper
nutmeg
4 eggs
2 oz. grated parmesan
2 cups whipping cream

Utensils

grater for cheese
mixing bowl
whisk
measuring spoons
measuring cup

Notes

Notes

Kitchen Photographs
and Descriptions

Kitchen Photographs and Descriptions

★ Dishwasher, oven and microwave safe
★ Clearly marked
★ Spout pours easily

★ Easy to read
★ Easy to pour
★ Microwave safe
★ Easy to grasp
★ Attractive enough to bring to the table
★ Breakable

All dishwasher safe

#1 Light, can get hand through handle

#2 4-cup measure - heavy particularly when filled with liquid

#3 Laboratory glass, easy to read, microwave safe

Available at gourmet shops, housewares and some large grocery stores

263

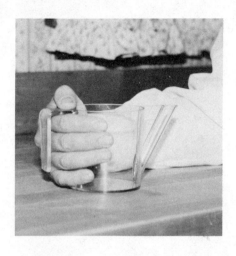

★ Flat of hand slides easily under handle
★ Pours from bottom so can be used to separate fat from gravy

★ Combination shaker and measuring cup
★ Closing must be played with a bit but not difficult
★ Excellent handle — entire hand fits through

#1 Unbreakable 1/2 cup and cup measure - light

#2 Professional quart measure large handle, unbreakable

#3 Plastic easy to read and pour

#4 See top picture

Measuring Cups

★ Very small handle
★ Must have a strong pinch to use it
★ Difficult to transfer liquids in for fragile hands
★ Can be hung on wall

★ Long handles
★ Easy to grasp
★ Can be hung on wall

★ Small plastic cups
★ Handle large enough to grasp
★ Cannot be hung on wall

★ Measuring spoons have easy to grasp handles
★ Bowl part of spoon easy to clean

★ Spoons taken off ring are easier to use than on ring
★ When one spoon is used - it is not then necessary to wash four spoons

★ Measuring cups hanging on wall make them accessible

★ These Tullen scissors from New Zealand are the greatest scissors to hit the market in years
★ They will cut almost anything
★ Spring handle makes cutting easy
★ Available with handy storage

Grater

★ Suction feet
★ Removable blades
★ Bin to catch food

Infusers

★ These are tea infusers
★ Herbs can be put inside instead of trying to tie a cheese cloth bag

Apple Sectioner

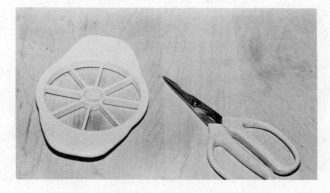

★ Comes in plastic and metal
★ Use two hands thus dividing the labor
★ Requires shoulder and arm strength

★ Large bulb whisk with good size handle makes it easy to hold and whip

★ Small battery-powered whisk will work for light tasks but not recommended for heavy-duty tasks

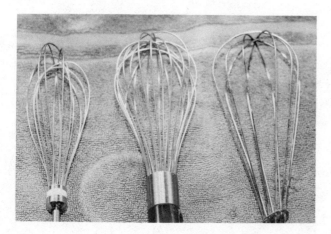

#1 Multipurpose whisk

#2 Good bulb will whip well

#3 Has few wires - will do better mixing rather than whipping

Whisks

There are many times that a beating motion must be performed in order to mix or whip the ingredients in a recipe. Whisks can be put into two groups, one hand operated and the other power operated. Hand whisks come in a variety of shapes and sizes. There are inexpensive whisks which have relatively few wires forming the bulb of the whisk and quite often come with a slender handle. These whisks would not be recommended for the disabled hand because in order to grasp the whisk the handle would need to be built up. Since the balloon part of the whisk has few wires it requires more beating to be done in performing the task.

There is however a professional whisk on the market that has a large stainless steel handle and a many wired bulb. This whisk is easy to hold and beat but is heavier than the slender handled whisk.

The battery operated whisks are either run by non-rechargeable batteries or come with a recharging stand. The electrical ones have a reasonable length cord. These whisks also vary in size, weight and durability.

Electric Kettle

* ★ Automatic turn off when empty
* ★ Speedy heating
* ★ Easy to pour
* ★ Saves motion of turning stove on and off
* ★ Whistle when ready
* ★ Has steam guard for hand

Heat Diffuser

* ★ Promotes even cooking
* ★ Lessens burning

Stove Top Cooking

* ★ Individual dinners may be cooked in this manner
* ★ Saves energy
* ★ Puts less heat into the kitchen thus keeping kitchen cooler in the summer

Two handled casseroles are easier to move than those without handles

★ Smaller broiling trays make cooking for one or two easier
★ Smaller area to clean up thus less fatigue

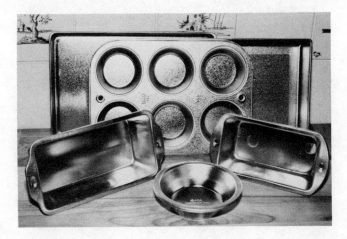

Toaster Oven Bake Set

★ Size geared to cooking for 1-2 people
★ Only drawback is they do not have non-stick surfaces

Two Piece Steamer with Lid

★ Handles easy to grasp
★ Steamer half lifts off easily
★ Washes easily

Folding Steamer

★ Fits most pots
★ Opens easily
★ Difficult for fragile hands to lift out of pot
★ No problem for strong hands

Scales

★ Portion control
★ Reduces wastage

★ An easy gadget to operate
★ With a simple motion size of opening can be regulated

★ To open jar no strong grip is required
★ Top of jar opens with lever principle

★ This little hat is made of rubber
★ Has ridges inside which grip top
★ Aids in opening jar but good grasp is still needed

Jar Openers

★ Both screw into the base of upper cabinet

★ Have teeth which grab the lid

★ Requires some strength in the hand to lift jar and turn jar

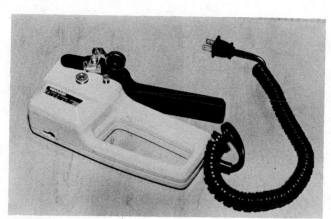

Electric Can Opener

★ Relatively light

★ Exceptionally easy to use

★ Takes some grasp to start

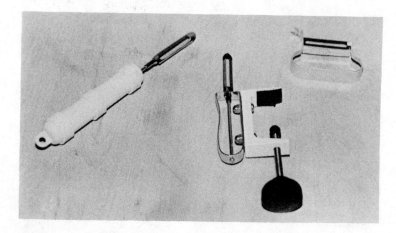

Peelers

1. Built up handle

2. Clamps on table top - you move the vegetable not the peeler

3. Whole hand fits through handle

Coffee Filter Dispenser

★ Lifts off one filter at a time

Thermos

★ Pump handle type no grip needed flat of hand will work
★ Put hot coffee in it in the morning — saves putting stove on and off thus less fatigue to the hand and less energy used

Acrylic Glasses

★ Light
★ Non-breakable
★ Come in many sizes shapes and styles

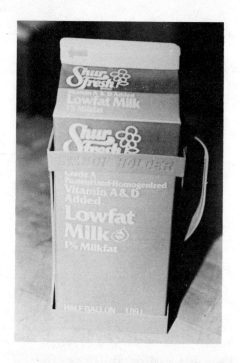

Milk Carton Handle

★ Makes lifting milk much easier
★ Carton steadier for pouring

Plastic Coated Clips

★ Must have some pinch to use
★ Much easier than twisties to get on and off

Pot Holder

★ Wraps around handle
★ Protects hand from bottom of pot

Handling Hot Objects

★ Pot holder fits handle of pot snugly
★ Makes moving pots with metal handles much safer
★ Comes in country fabrics

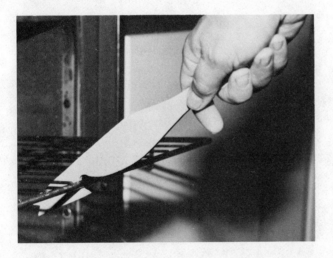

★ A wonderful old-fashioned means of pulling out and pushing in oven racks

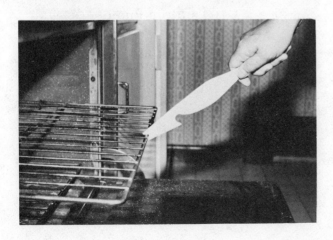

★ Long handled tools are a must for barbecuing
★ Large easy to grip handles

Electric Barbecue Starter

★ Starting charcoal fires is safe and easy
★ Takes about 10 minutes to start coals
★ Much safer for fragile hands than liquid starter

Catsup Pump

★ Pump can be used with the flat of hand
★ No taking top of bottle off and on

Lazy Susan

★ A simple inexpensive solution to storing can goods

Mixing Bowls

★ Have non-skid ring built into base
★ Light to lift
★ Left and center bowl have minimal handle
★ Right bowl has easy to grasp handle

Two Handled Knife

★ Excellent for cutting cheese and anything else that is resistive to cutting
★ Two handles divide the work load between hands

Knives

1. Chef's knife
2. Bread knife with serrated edges
3. Fillet knife
4. Teflon coated knife will not stain such things as eggplant
5. Small Japanese utility knife

Serrated Carving Knife

Next three knives - old knives - their shape is due to years of sharpening

Knife 5 general purpose knife

Knife 6 a serrated small knife

Knife 7 a tomato knife with fork on end

Knife 8 common knife cannot be easily sharpened

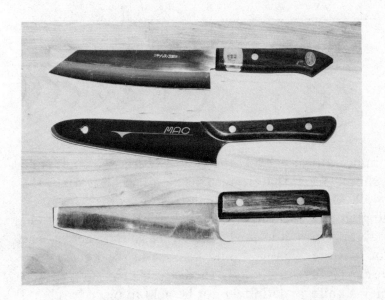

1. Very sharp chopping knife

2. Well balanced knife no point
   with which to get stuck

3. Large rocker knife - well
   balanced easy to handle

Knives

Knives are one of the most important tools that a cook has. They should be treated with great care and respect. Most knives do not survive washing in the dishwasher nor do they like soaking. On page 290 you can see how not to store your knives. A top quality knife can last a lifetime so it is important to pick a knife that fits your hand well and does the work you want it to.

There are three parts to a knife - blade, tang and handle. The blades are designed to do various kinds of cutting, chopping, slicing, carving and boning. The blades are made from steel and stainless steel. The three famous steels are Shefield, Sollingen and Sabatier. These names do not always mean top quality knives. It most often depends upon who made the knife. For instance about twelve different firms make Sabatier knives. They pay for the privilege of using that name. I feel it is best to choose a knife for the job you want it to do. Good knives are not going to be cheap or reasonable as the case may be.

The tang is an extension of the blade that fits into the handle. This is where the balance of the knife comes from. A poorly balanced knife does not feel right and can be a hazard as it is tip heavy. The tang should be held in the handle with preferably three rivets. The tang should definitely not be held in place by glue. I have seen several knives by different companies break where the blade becomes the tang. The tang should not be thin - so check for thickness.

The handle can be made from wood, plastic, very hard rubber, rose-wood and stainless steel. The slick handles can be hard to hold onto as can handles that have been made to conform to finger indentions. This is fine if your hand is the same size as the one for which the handle was made. However more often than not the hand will not fit. Check the handle carefully to be sure it fits your hand comfortably.

Safety Factors When Handling Knives

1. Always work with sharp knives
2. Do not put a knife on the edge of the counter where it could easily fall off and cut your feet
3. Do not put knives loose in a drawer as you can cut yourself searching in the drawer
4. Do not throw a knife in a sink that is filled with soapy water as you will not know where that knife is and could get easily cut

A Few Don'ts Concerning Knives

1. Don't put your knife in the dishwasher
2. Don't hold knives in a flame
3. Don't use a knife as a lid opener
4. Don't dip knives into a pot with simmering food
5. Don't use a lightweight knife to do a heavy task
6. Don't use a cooking knife to open packages
7. Don't store knifes in a drawer loose
8. Don't soak knives

A Few Do's About Knives

1. Do sharpen knives frequently
2. Do wash and dry knives as soon as they have been used
3. Do enjoy the beauty of a well made knife that is capable of doing the job it was designed to do

Some of the knives that would be useful to you are:

1. Chef's knife
2. Paring knife
3. Boning knife if your hands are strong enough
4. Carving knife
5. Bread knife
6. Serrated knife for food like tomatoes

REMEMBER A KNIFE IS AN EXTENSION OF YOUR HAND

Knife Sharpener

★ Rolling motion on table
★ Roll on one side of sharpener then the other
★ A two step method

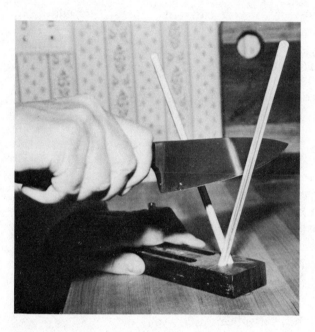

Knife Sharpener

★ Downward motion on first one side then the other
★ Does not take much strength
★ A two step job

Knife Sharpener

★ Pulling motion
★ Hold base with one hand or clamp
★ One step motion

Manual Chopper

★ Can be used with the flat of hand
★ Does take arm and shoulder strength

Food Processor

★ Controls can be run with little pressure
★ Feeding tube can be pressed with flat of hand
★ Bowl has easy to grasp handle
★ Models that have stem and disc separate can be difficult to snap together for fragile hands
★ Many models come with discs and stems as one piece
★ A food processor can change your life in the kitchen from a nightmare to a delight
★ Food processors are made by many companies - choose the one that is easiest for you to use
★ Do not buy one unless you have tried to put it together and take it apart

Carts

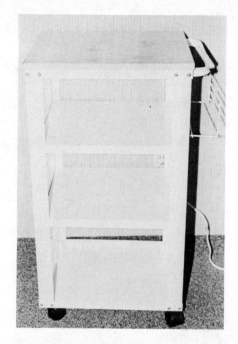

★ This cart has butcher block top
★ Metal pegboard on side for utensils or pots
★ Two shelves
★ Rolls easily
★ Handle makes pushing easy

Pull Down Cookbook Rack

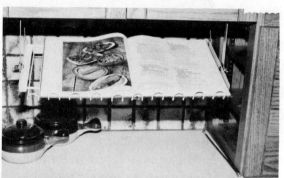

★ Keeps book off counter
★ At a height that is easy to read
★ Folds up under counter when through

Glass Cleaner

★ Suction feet
★ Push glasses over bristles

Pottery Counter Storage

★ Slides easily
★ Tops remove easily
★ Too heavy for fragile hands to lift

Counter Storage

★ Jars keep moisture out
★ Easy to see what is in jar
★ No wasted motions look-ing in containers to see what you have
★ If there is a problem with opening, the clasp can be popped up with the handle of a spoon

Canister

★ See through
★ Push button seal and release top
★ Keeps moisture out
★ Comes in decorator colors

Proper storage of herbs is very important.
They should not be exposed to LIGHT or AIR.

#1 Pottery storage - corks
remove easily

#2 Plastic storage

★ Top removes easily
★ Container light

#3 Metal tins are light
★ Lids remove easily

#4 Glass spice jars lying flat in
drawer
★ Labels up easy to read

#1

#2

#3

#4

#1 Old copper kettle used as utensil storage

#2 Carousel - turns thus making utensils accessible no rummaging means less fatigue

#3 Measuring spoons stored singly in cup on counter

#4 Knife storage on counter
★ Knives protected

A Simple Manner of Storing Knives

★ Attached to the wall
★ Does not take up counter space
★ Easy to make
★ Knives accessible and ready to use

★ Keeps knives separated from each other
★ Helps knives retain their sharpness
★ Easy to lift knives out

★ Do you store your knives this way?
★ An absolute NO-NO
★ Knives get dull
★ You get cut

Herbs in Metal Containers on Shelf

★ Very accessible
★ Tea tins in single layer
★ One motion gets tea or herbs

Overhead Storage of Glasses

★ Works well if shoulders function normally
★ Cups on shelf over sink
★ Easy access to both glasses and cups

Open Shelf Over Windows

★ Storage area for SELDOM used bowls
★ Relieves accessible spaces of bowls used once a year

Small Metal Pot Rack

★ No lifting of many pots to get one pot
★ Decorative attractive manner of storing pots

Excellent Open Accessible Storage

★ Pot rack on wall
★ Spice rack out
★ Utensils in bucket
★ Large salt shaker on stove

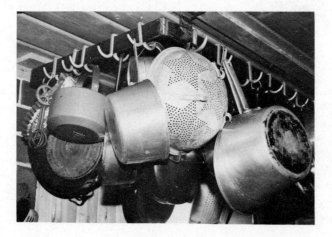

Commercial Pot Rack

★ Holds a great deal
★ Good vertical storage
★ Ideal for serious cooks

Open Shelves

★ Attractive storage containers on counter

★ Lack of doors cuts down fatiguing motion

★ Open cabinets can be attractive
★ Think of it as a china hutch

★ A workmanlike counter and shelves with everything handy
★ Cups on cup hooks
★ Chopping boards ready to be used
★ Utensils in crock
★ Food processor ready and waiting
★ Flour and sugar tubs out and available

Open shelves with a bit of dressing up

Storage Containers for the Refrigerator

Some containers work very well for those with two strong hands but if fragile hands attempt to open the container it becomes a tussle and certainly stress is put on the joints. The weight of the container should be considered: if the container is made from heavy pottery and then filled with food it will of course become very heavy which will contribute to the fatigue factor. A jar that has clear sides obviously does not have to be picked up or have the lid unscrewed in order to find out what is inside thus conserving energy.

If a dishwasher is available then it certainly is easier on the hands to have the dishwasher wash the container rather than do it by hand. We all have storage problems in our kitchen so it is a bonus if the container can have more than one job - such as the ability to serve or cook from as well as store. The size of the container is important i.e. a pint of soup stores better in a pint jar than in a quart jar.

The storage containers for the refrigerator mentioned in this book have been tested with the following criterea in mind.

1. Can I put the top on and off with ease causing little or no stress on the joints?

2. Can I see through the container?

3. Will the container hold up in the dishwasher?

4. How durable is the container - will it crack, break or chip easily.

5. Are the containers a useful size?

6. If the containers are for pouring do they pour easily?

7. How heavy is the container?

8. Can the container go from freezer to oven?

9. Can the container be used for freezing without getting freezer burn?

★ If you must transfer one cup of boiling water or stock pour it into a TWO cup measure
★ This prevents boiling liquid sloshing out

★ To ease stress on hands slide casserole from counter to stove

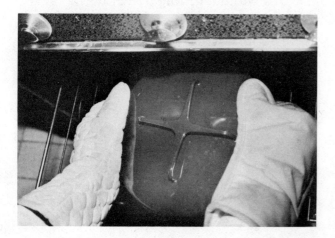

★ Use TWO hands to remove casserole from oven
★ Wear good mitts not damaged or WET ones

★ When doing many dishes by hand sit down at the sink
★ Open cabinet doors below sink and rest feet on cabinet floor
★ A back to the stool eases fatigue

★ When washing pots, pans and dishes try to do the task with the hand in a flat position

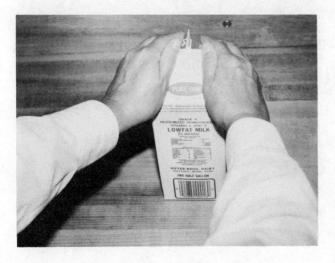

★ Opening milk cartons can be a tough task
★ Push opening back with BOTH hands
★ Slip DULL knife between paper layers and pry open

Stabilization of Mixing Bowls

★ Dycem, a sticky fabric which keeps bowls and plates in their place
★ Does not mar finish

Available at nautical supply houses, R.V. supply houses

★ Hold bowl between legs and mix

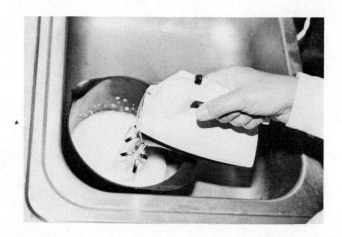

★ Put bowl in corner of sink when mixing by hand or with a hand mixer

★ Pliers can be used to remove the tab from a juice can

★ Removing the paper tab from a juice can
★ Pliers grasp the tab easily
★ Roll pliers with the tab and the pliers do the work

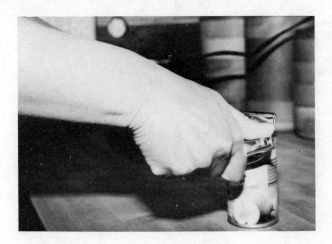

★ A traditional can opener, while fine for the strong hand, can put stress on finger joints, thumb and the wrist

Filling Seal-a-Bag Boilable Pouches

★ Put bag in measuring cup
★ Ladle food into bag
★ Using ladle reduces stress on the hand

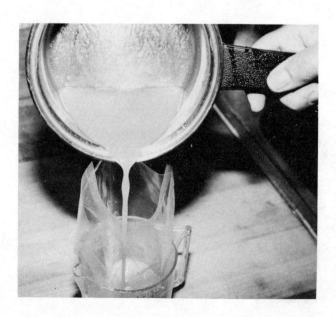

★ Put bag in measuring cup
★ Pour soup from pan into bag ONLY if pan is light
★ Too heavy a pan will cause stress on the hand and wrist

Sealing Food

★ Insert open edge of boilable pouch in sealer
★ Push sealing bar with flat of hand
★ Hold down for desired length of time
★ Remove bag

★ This Small tool opens any sealed plastic bag with a sliding motion

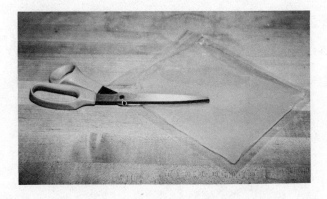

★ Good scissors are an easy, safe way to open plastic bags and food wrapped in plastic

★ Never open a plastic bag with a knife

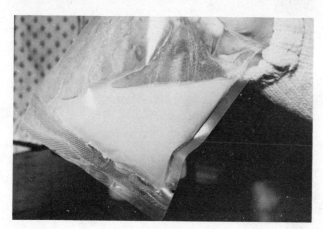

★ Bags sealed in this manner hold liquid tightly
★ Reduce chance of freezer burn
★ Boilable pouches cut down on clean up thus causing less fatigue

302

★ Sifting flour without having to squeeze a sifter
★ Slowly scrape a spoon through the flour — rubbing flour through strainer

★ Whisking can be done either with the arm in this position or with the wrist locked

★ Peeling hard cooked eggs can be frustrating when eggs are very fresh
★ Slip spoon under membrane and flick off shell

★ Plastic grater is easy to hold
★ Rub egg over grater with flat of hand

★ Fine grating on steel grater
★ Long handle
★ Rub egg over grater with the flat of hand

Grated egg over salads manages to turn a rather ordinary looking salad into a work of art

★ Making bread crumbs
★ Put stale bread in plastic bag
★ Seal with clip
★ Roll over plastic bag with a rolling pin with no handles
★ Use the flat of hand to perform motion

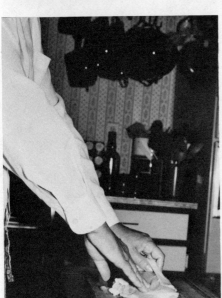

★ This picture shows work being done at the INCORRECT height
★ If work surface is too low then the tendency is to bend over thus causing fatigue in both the back, neck and shoulders

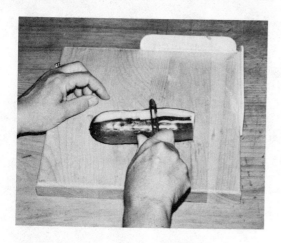

★ Put lip of board away from you
★ Push cucumber through nail using caution to always keep fingers away from nails
★ Peel top of cucumber
★ Remove cucumber and replace on nails to reach other parts of cucumber

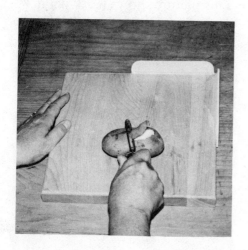

★ Do likewise with potato
★ Always peel with motion towards thumb side

★ Do likewise with carrot

* Adaptive cutting board
* Corner lips to hold bread while buttering
* Can easily be made BUT ONLY USE STAINLESS NAILS

* Adaptive cutting board has stainless nails protruding through board
* Nails hold what needs to be peeled or sliced

* Chicken breast held securely on nails
* Cutting chicken breast into finger length strips

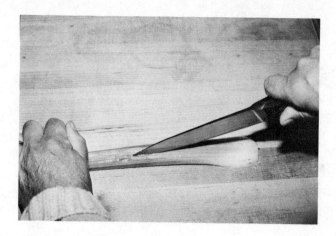

★ Lay rib of celery on chopping board

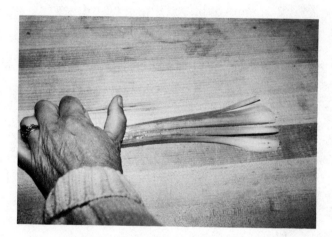

★ Slice lengthwise 4-5 times

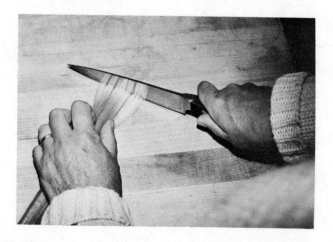

★ Chop across slices
★ This method reduces amount of chopping time thus reduces fatigue

★ Roughly chopped celery

★ Diced celery

★ Minced celery

★ Slice white part of green onion
   lengthwise 3-4 times

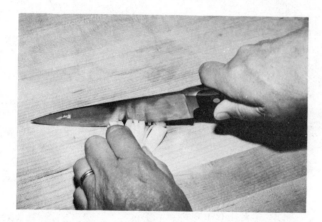

★ Cut across green onion

★ Then chop
★ This method reduces amount
   of chopping time thus reduces
   fatigue

Chopping with a Chef's knife

★ With left hand resting on back of knife above pointed end — raise knife handle with right hand

★ Keeping left hand in same position bring knife handle down with right hand letting the knife do the work

★ Keeping left hand in same position bring knife handle up with right hand

★ Pulling the vegetables toward you into a pile with the blade of the knife

★ With blade of knife scrape vegetables into a pile from the right side locking the wrist

★ Then do the same from the left side
★ When vegetables are in a pile one motion goes through many vegetables
★ When vegetables are spread out it takes much more energy to do the same task

★ Keep scraping the vegetables into a pile

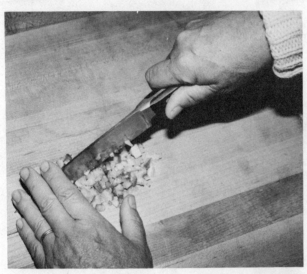

★ Then proceed to chop

★ Scrape into a pile

★ Vegetables in this picture are being finely diced

★ When finished lift the diced vegetables with the blade of the knife and put into a bowl

★ Upper cabinet pantry with swing out interiors

★ Easy to find what is needed with shallow shelves

★ Larger items can be put at the back of the cabinet

★ Pantry cabinet with single loading
★ Upper part of cabinet swings out
★ No lifting of cans while searching for what is needed

★ Metal coated rack that screws onto door to house light objects

★ Tray shelves that screw onto doors adding more vertical single depth storage

★ Wooden spice racks that swing out

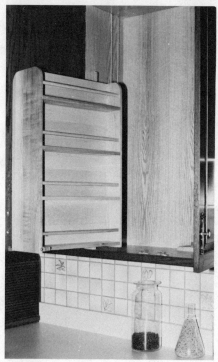

★ These swing out shelves allow depth storage of spices leaving area in back for larger items
★ Spices also are in the dark which makes them last longer

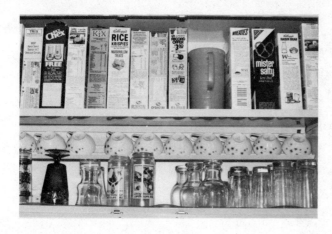

★ Regular cabinets with doors removed providing easy accessibility to glasses and dishes

★ Regular cabinets with doors removed providing easy accessibility to glasses and dishes

★ Corner cabinet that will open full
★ No need to reach around objects

318

Upper corner cabinets with no wasted corners

★ Storage of flatware and small utensils does best when there are dividers
★ Less rooting around and searching

★ An extra work surface has been slipped under the utensil drawer

★ A utensils drawer should be easy to clean and wipe out

Garages to store small appliances. Tambour openings
can be adjusted to open easily. These garages while a
luxury do keep a kitchen looking less cluttered.

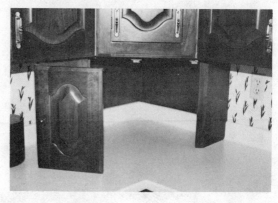

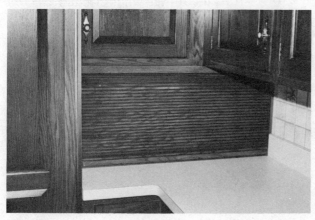

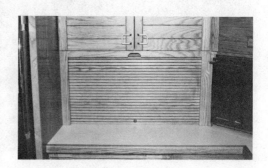

★ Microwave at good height
★ No sliding area to microwave which could cause a safety problem if something heavy needs to be removed from oven

★ Microwave with good space around it

★ A simple solution to lack of counter space around oven
★ Pull out bread board doubles as a counter when needed

★ Ovens built in at the proper height reduce fatigue
★ Ovens at an incorrect height can cause accidents due to the position you are in while removing food from the oven
★ If building in a single oven — have the middle of the oven at counter height

★ Good cabinet hardware
★ Maximum counter space around appliances

★ Desk in kitchen saves steps
★ Can keep an eye on food while sitting down at the desk

★ Trash compactor keeps trash
   out of sight
★ When full can be heavy
★ Good task for spouse or neigh-
   bor to help empty

★ Small appliances garage has
   plenty of sliding room
   around it
★ Lower corner cabinet utilizes
   corner dead space
★ Good cabinet hardware

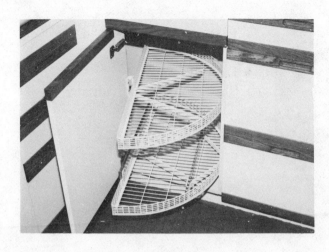

★ Plastic coated wire shelves swing then pull out
★ Good size lip

★ Deep lip that holds pots and casseroles in

★ Triple shelved unit enables you to NOT have to stack
★ No lifting of one object to get at another

Lower Base Corner Cabinet

★ Deep lip
★ Shelves swing individually

★ This picture is the same as above but in stationary position

★ Swing out shelves which go back into the corner
★ Good use of dead space

Lower Base Corner Cabinet

★ Small lip on sides
★ Shelves turn individually

★ These shelves rotate like a
  lazy susan

★ Swing out corner cabinet with
  shelves attached to the door

Lower Cabinet Corner Cabinets

* ★ Door attached to shelves
* ★ Shelves do not move individually

* ★ With no lip on sides objects can fall off as shelf is spun around
* ★ Door opens and you reach in

* ★ Door jointed in center opens full
* ★ Shelves turn individually

★ A Deep sided drawer which will hold two baskets for separating trash

★ This basket slides easily in and out and can be easily lifted out for cleaning

★ Above basket comes out when door is opened and simultaneously the lid raises

★ Basket on arm to slide out
★ This method works but not as smoothly as built in baskets

★ Wire basket for 3 waste baskets where separating trash is a necessity

★ A tilt waste basket should have a handle on the cabinet allowing all of the fingers to slip through

★ Two pull out baskets both roll in and out easily

★ Slide out drawers make stored items much easier to reach
★ Less bending over of the body
★ Less moving of objects to get at things stored in back of shelf
★ The whole kitchen does not have to be this way but most used items should be sorted in this manner
★ An excellent way of storing small utensils
★ Saves motion
★ No need to root around

★ A nice luxury — saves counter space

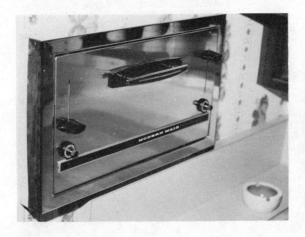

Lower Cabinet Storage

Lower pull out drawer
sectioned off in wood for
pop or liquor

★ Lower cabinet storage sectioned
off with wire for soda or liquor

★ A storage area for pans
★ Sectioning off reduces need to
move a lot of pans to get to the
one needed

★ Slide out for under the sink
★ Makes soaps more accessible

★ Slide out can storage
★ Takes up little room
★ When cans are stored doubly
  — cans must be lifted to see what you have
★ This manner suitable for end of cabinets

★ Cans stored on both sides
★ This type suitable anywhere in base cabinet line except corners

The Cadillac of the Industry

★ Every item is where you can see it
★ Every item is stored at a single depth

Instant Hot Water Faucet

★ Economical to run
★ No knobs to turn
★ Faucet operated by the flat of hand
★ Easy to make coffee and instant soups

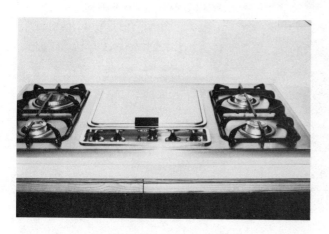

★ Knobs on front are a strong safety factor
★ No reaching across steaming pots to regulate heat

★ Lower work surface for rolling dough
★ This is very important for those who roll baked goods
★ Incorrect height can cause undue back, shoulder and neck fatigue

#1 and #2 Heavy duty chopping
block tucked away

#3 Storage for scouring pads
and soap in front of sink
★ Good handles

#4 Storage for crackers and
bread
★ Cleans easily

★ Tray and pan storage
★ Partitions recessed at top which makes getting at needed pan easier
★ This cabinet located above built in oven which might be too high for some people

Cart

★ Has storage place of its own
★ Can easily be pulled out

★ Carts do a great deal to take the stress off hands and arms
★ Be sure wheels are satisfactory and do not have trouble going over cords and rug edges

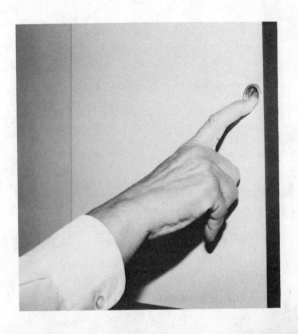

★ This means of opening a cabinet puts tremendous stress on the fingers

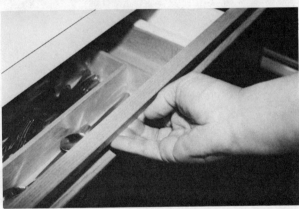

★ This type of drawer opening is no problem for the strong hand but hard on the fragile hand

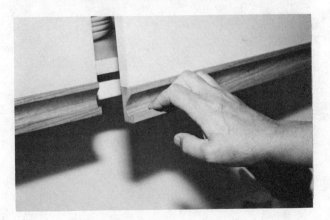

★ This type of cabinet opening is no problem for the strong hand but hard on the fragile hand

★ Hardware that permits the whole hand to slide through is the least damaging to finger joints

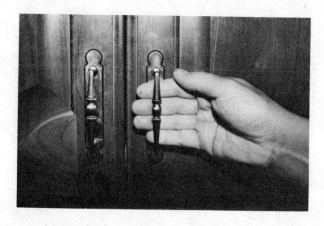

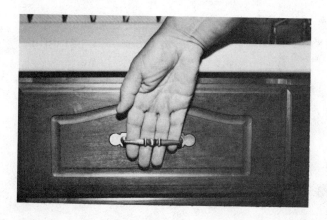

★ Combination eating and work areas
★ Note two different table heights
★ Excellent cabinet hardware

★ Easily cleaned cabinet doors
★ Gooseneck faucet makes pans easier to clean
★ Attractive eating and work area not crowding the stove and sink
★ Open storage for cups

A beautifully designed kitchen with eating/prep area not interfering with stove and sink. Several people can work in this kitchen without getting in each other's way

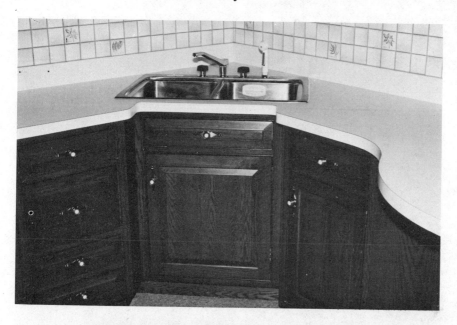

★ A galley kitchen saves steps
which in turn cuts down on
fatigue
★ Garage at end of kitchen keeps
small appliances out of sight

★ Cabinet hardware easy to
operate
★ Counter space around microwave makes oven easy to
operate

The following companies graciously allowed me to photograph their lovely, efficient and desirable kitchens for which I greatly thank you.

KITCHENS by KRENGEL, INC.,
St. Paul, Minnesota
Carrying the following companies
RUTT
WOODMODE
CRYSTAL

KITCHENS UNIQUE, Edina, Minnesota
Carrying the following companies
FIELDSTONE
MIDDLECREEK
RICHMAID

ST. CHARLES KITCHENS,
Edina, Minnesota

Hints and Tips

Hints and Tips

You and Your Kitchen

How does work in the kitchen get accomplished?
* ★ Who cooks which meals?
* ★ Who does meal clean up?
* ★ Do you prefer to cook and clean up with others?
* ★ How many people use the kitchen together?
* ★ Is the present division of labor satisfactory?

How many cooks should your kitchen accommodate at once?
How many people are served daily?
How many meals are served daily?
How often do you have guests?
How many guests do you have at one time?

Kitchen Habits

Do you mind having kitchen mess be seen?
Do you like to visit in the kitchen?
Do your children do their homework in the kitchen?
Do you like to eat in the kitchen?
Is your kitchen really the family center?

Hints and Tips on Kitchen Habits

It is important to always keep jars and dry foods in the same place. For instance always store the mayonnaise in the same place in the refrigerator — then YOU know where it is and unnecessary items do not have to be moved to get at the mayonnaise. If someone helps you clean out the refrigerator have a chart made up ahead of time showing where everything goes. This chart can be put on the refrigerator door and guests and other members of the family can use it as a guide.

Be sure you have a comfortable place to unload the groceries. A place to put groceries as soon as you come in the door is helpful. Also counter space near the refrigerator and near the storage for canned goods.

Try to have your kitchen door as close to the car as possible. If you live in an apartment or condo you can use a folding cart to wheel the groceries into your place.

Traffic patterns — try to banish routine household traffic from your work area. It is exhausting and irritating to keep getting out of the way while a member of the family walks by. Have your work area away from the back door if at all possible.

Duplicate some small utensils and staples. For instance have one set of measuring cups and spoons at your "food prep area" and another set and color near the stove. Then when you are cleaning up you will know exactly where each measuring cup goes because it is color coded to the area in which it is used. Duplicate the flour and salt also. This way you do not need to move from one area to another. If you continually avoid wasted motion you will protect your joints and lessen fatigue.

To Lessen Fatigue

Do not stay at any one task for an extended time. If you can alternate between a standing task and a sitting one you will become less tired.

While standing to do a task — open the bottom cabinet door and rest one foot on the shelf. Alternate which foot you put on the shelf every few minutes. A brass bar can be put on the outside of the cabinet door for resting your foot — if the door is strong enough to carry the weight.

If you can learn how to handle a chef's knife properly it will save you much fatigue. A chef's knife should be used while standing working at the proper height. If you sit down and chop the task will take two to three times as long and your body will be out of line. Stand and do the job and it will be done quickly and efficiently.

The most efficient and easy to reach storage is 18" - 20" off the floor to approximately 60" off the floor. This is for someone 5'4" -5'6" tall. Adapt that efficient space to your height.

Table height while sitting at work — I have found that working at a table about two inches lower than the normal eating height lessens my fatigue. Somehow the usual height gets my shoulders and neck out of kilter. It may not work for you but it saves me from back pain.

Rolling carts: These will help you take the stress off your joints and cut down on your fatigue. If your kitchen has the space by all means use it. Plan your clearance around tables and counters to accommodate the cart. Find a handy place to store it out of the way or incorporate it in to your overall kitchen design.

Organizing Your Kitchen

There are several ways to tackle the problem of kitchen organization. I think the best results are obtained when you ask yourself some questions and divide the kitchen into areas.

What type of cooking do I like best to do?
1. baking
2. desserts
3. appetizers
4. grilling
5. sauces
6. main dishes

Think of your kitchen as divided into areas
What area means the most to me?
1. cook center
2. clean up center
3. bake center
4. storage/pantry area
5. prep area

Is entertaining a part of my life?
How do I like to entertain?
1. dessert and coffee
2. drinks and appetizers
3. small dinners
4. buffets
5. picnics and barbecues

Can I tolerate others in the kitchen helping?
1. ahead of time
2. getting the food on the table and cleaning up

Let's take the kitchen now in areas.

Cook Center — Over All

The following is a list of what might be included in that area depending upon the type of cooking you do and what is comfortable for you.

★ Stove either counter top or with oven

- ★ Ovens either wall or part of stove
- ★ Storage for roasting pans
- ★ Storage for pots and pans
- ★ Storage for casserole dishes
- ★ Storage for cooking utensils
- ★ Storage for lids
- ★ Location of microwave
- ★ Location of toaster oven
- ★ Pot holders
- ★ Counter top near stove
- ★ Ability to slide pots to stove

Stoves

The kind of stove you have will ultimately be determined by the type of power available to you. I am not going to get into brands and which one I feel will work better. Instead I am going to list certain guidelines in question form that I think should be considered before purchasing a stove.

Questions

- ★ Are the knobs easy to turn?
- ★ Are the knobs easily accessible?
- ★ Do you have rapid control over the heating element if it is electrical?
- ★ Is the stove top easy to clean or does it have areas that can catch food?
- ★ If electrical is there a place to put a pot if you no longer want food cooking either on the stove or a heat resistant counter top?

Discussion of Questions

1. If the knobs are at the back of the stove they may be difficult to turn off when pots are on all the burners. This could cause steam burns. Cook tops often come with knobs on the side, in front or in the center. Slide in stoves are very difficult to find with knobs in the front. Drop in stoves do come with knobs in the front.

2. If you do not have rapid control over the heating element you can easily burn food, have the milk boil over or just generally over cook the food.

3. Some stove tops are a real bear to clean. The whole top comes off as a unit and then where do you put it after you get it off? Other stoves have a flat top so they do not catch food as easily. There are drip pans that are coated with a non-stick surface that make cleaning easier.

4. If you cook for a lot of people you need to be sure there is a place to put a pot which must come off the stove. If there is an unused burner free then there is no problem but when all burners are in use then there is a problem. Be sure you have a heat resistant surface next to the stove.

Ovens

The ideal height for an oven is to have the center of the oven the same height as the counter. This obviously avoids strain on the back and makes the transporting of food from the oven to the counter safer. However, we cannot always have what is ideal.

Questions

- ★ Do you like self-cleaning ovens?
- ★ Do you like continuous cleaning ovens?
- ★ Do you mainly broil?
- ★ Do you mainly bake?
- ★ How many do you normally cook for excluding holidays?
- ★ Do you know about probes?

Discussion of Questions

1. Self-cleaning ovens save a tremendous

amount of wear and tear on the hands not to mention almost the entire body. They do cost more and it takes power to do the cleaning but well worth it.

2. Some continuous cleaning ovens never really get clean. Some also have a finish on the oven that makes it hard to clean.

3. Broiling is difficult to do in gas stoves. The broiler is below the oven which means that you either have to bend way over to tend the food or kneel on the floor. Neither is a good position for the body.

4. Baking is really fine in either a regular oven or the top of a two-oven stove. Roasting normally means weight so be sure you do not have to bend too low to remove the roast from the oven.

5. The size of your oven should be geared to the normal amount of cooking that you do. If you are by yourself then it is pointless to heat up a large oven everyday. Perhaps a toaster oven for everyday use would make sense and the large oven when you are cooking for guests.

6. Probes are a great invention. You insert the probe into the roast or turkey and plug the other end into the monitor. You then set the probe dial for how well you like your meat cooked and it does the rest. Perfectly done meat everytime.

Microwave Ovens

The microwave oven should be at counter height like any other oven.

Questions

★ Is the kind of cooking I do adaptable to microwave cooking?

★ Is fast cooking an advantage to me?

★ Can I put the microwave in an accessible spot?

★ Is it possible to have a firm pull out shelf in front of the microwave?

Discussion of Questions

1. Microwave ovens do not handle baked goods well. They also do not cook roasts and poultry in the same manner as a conventional oven. They are excellent for cooking fish and vegetables and reheating dinners.

2. They do cook in far less time than conventional ovens and use less power, thus are quite economical to run. However, they do not take the place of a regular oven. They are used in addition to a conventional oven.

3. Microwaves should be put where they are easy to use. Some kitchen designs have stashed them where they may look attractive but it is difficult to use them.

4. Solid pull out shelves just below the microwave are a great addition both as a safety factor and for joint protection.

Convection Ovens

Convection ovens are not related to the microwave ovens. A convection oven is built in a similar fashion to a regular oven, however it has a fan built into it. The fan moves the air around the oven thus preventing hot spots. It also means that the food is cooked in an even manner and in less time. It browns and does an incredible job roasting meats. There is much less shrinkage so the meat does not get dried out. I do not recommend Yorkshire pudding being cooked in this oven. Hurriedly one Christmas I popped the pudding in the oven, pushed the buttons and went into the living room to join my guests. I went back into the kitchen about 15 minutes later and found the Yorkshire pudding in peaks at the four corners of the pan. It resembled a crown. It was a funny sight. The fan had caused the problem. However it was delicious. I have had no problem with souffles and quiches. Perhaps that is because the pans are round.

Questions

★ Do I roast and bake a lot?
★ Is shortening the cooking time important?
★ Is it possible to have a pull out shelf in front of the convection oven?
★ Is continuous cleaning important?

Discussion of Questions

1. The oven does a superb job on all roasting jobs. The baking is also handled in a first rate manner. If you cook a lot this oven is definitely a great asset. It is usually a little larger than the average microwave and considerably smaller than a regular oven.

2. It cooks more quickly than a regular oven and less quickly than a microwave.

3. A pull out shelf below the convection oven is a great advantage as you can slide a heavy roast from the oven to the shelf and then obtain a good grip and put the roast where you want it.

Toaster Ovens

Toaster ovens come in many sizes and abilities to do the job. There are small not particularly well insulated ones that are fine for English muffins and broiled sandwiches but are just not heavy duty enough to economically cook meals. The larger well insulated ones can bake and broil in just about the same time as a regular oven and are pretty economical to run when compared to a regular oven.

Questions

★ Do I have counter space for it?
★ How easy are the knobs to turn?
★ How large a meal do I usually cook?
★ How many do I cook for?

Discussion of Questions

1. Counter space is usually a precious commodity so it is important to determine whether a toaster oven has priority or if space is very limited whether something else such as a food processor should be considered first?

2. If you cook for a family and have several things to put in the oven for dinner then a toaster oven would not be efficient for you.

3. If you live alone and usually heat up one item for an entree and perhaps steam your vegetables then perhaps a toaster oven is for you.

Roasting Pans and Baking Pans

Questions

★ Is it difficult to reach overhead to store them?
★ Can I bend down to put them in a lower cabinet?
★ Do I have space to separate pans so that I do not have to lift three pans to get at one pan?
★ How many pans do I really need to get at on a daily basis?

Discussion of Questions

1. On page 336 you will see overhead storage. Usually you need to be tall to easily get the pans down. If the pans are put inside each other and stored at that height they can come

crashing down on your head when taken out of storage.

2. The pans in a lower cabinet as in page 332 are another way to store pans. They certainly are easier to reach at this level in a pull out drawer.

3. Anytime you have to move pans to get at the one you want, you are abusing your hands. Each wasted motion adds to the fatigue process. Try to store your pans so that one single movement will do the job.

4. Take inventory of your pans separating them into a pile of daily use, weekly use and seldom used. The large roasting pan is seldom used so that pan should be stored in an area that is not premium space. If you bake bread weekly put those pans in an accessible spot. I think you will be surprised what few pans you use on a weekly basis.

Storage of Pots and Pans

Questions

★ Is pulling a sliding drawer out difficult?
★ Do I have room to hang them on the wall?
★ Can I easily put my arms over my head and lift a pot down?
★ Is there a way to store them so that they are not nesting in each other?

Discussion of Questions

1. If you have the room sliding shelves or drawers are an easy way to store pots as long as you do not put the pots inside each other.

2. Hanging pots on the wall means a single motion is needed to get the pots down which saves energy and avoids joint abuse.

3. If you can easily put your arms over your head and have a high enough ceiling then the pot racks could be the answer for you. However do not pile lots of pots on the same hook or you defeat one of the purposes of the pot rack. The other advantage of a pot rack is the use of vertical space. If you have a small kitchen then the only extra space may be up.

4. There are ways of storing pots in a lower cabinet on a stand that separates each pot. To store frequently used pots a lower cabinet means a lot of bending over and deep knee bends. You might consider finding a place to hang, either on a grid or peg board, the most frequently used pots and store the rest in a lower cabinet.

Pot Lids

The bane of a cook's existance is pot lids. The amount of energy that is used trying to find the right lid for the right pan is amazing.

Questions

★ Do I have room to put them in a sliding drawer?
★ Is there a place to store them on the wall?
★ Do I have room for a lid rack?
★ Can they be stored on top of each pot?

Discussion of Questions

1. There are some drawers that come equipped with a special lid rack that keeps the lids separated. The lids and pots could be color coded with adhesive colored labels which would then tell you which top belonged with which pan.

2. Storing the lids next to the pots on the wall is a magical way of keeping the right lid with the right pot.

3. There are lid racks that can be put in a pantry storage area. They are made out of plastic coated wire. These will work provided there is enough clearance room above the basket to get the lid out.

4. If you have a lot of space they can be stored on top of a pot and the pots kept in a single layer in a sliding drawer.

Casseroles

Questions

★ Do I like having casseroles out on open shelves?
★ Is there a place for an open cupboard to house the casseroles?
★ Will a slide out drawer be too heavy with casseroles in it?

Discussion of Questions

1. Casseroles that are out on open shelves can look very attractive. They also can collect grease and dirt if not used regularly.

2. Often at the end of the cupboard that juts out into the room there is space to store some casseroles.

3. Casseroles usually do not stack well and if they did nest that would require extra motion to get at the casserole you need. If the slide out shelf is not too large you should easily be able to slide the drawer in and out with the casseroles in a single layer

Small Cooking Utensils

Questions

★ Do I have space to put them in drawers with dividers?
★ Would I rather have then in a con-

tainer on the counter?
★ Is it easier for me to work from a peg board or a grid?

Discussion of Questions

1. If you opt to put the wooden spoons, slotted spoons and spatulas in a drawer be sure they are put in a sizable drawer with dividers. Rummaging around in a drawer for a particular utensil is a lot of grasping of this and that which you do not want to do.

2. Storing small utensils in a carousel or a container on the counter is an excellent way of having your most used utensils at your fingertips. See page 289. It needn't look cluttered. If you cook a lot it is the most sensible way to go.

3. Pegboards and now plastic-coated metal grids are another way of keeping things out in the open within easy reach. It does require wall space and is fine in a large kitchen but might be a space problem in a small kitchen. Pegboards can also be mounted inside a cabinet and then pulled out. See page 331.

Pot Holders

Pot holders should be hung within easy reach of the stove or oven. Putting pot holders in a drawer out of sight means that every time you need a pot holder you also have to open and close the drawer. Once again wasted motion.

Counter Tops

Questions

★ Do I need the counter top heat resistant?
★ Do I need the counter top water-proof?

★ Do I need to chop on the counter?

Discussion of Questions

1. If you cook a lot thus having all burners of the stove going you need a heat resistant counter top near the stove. Corian does the job beautifully. It is expensive but lasts a very long time.

2. Around the sink it is a good idea to have the counter waterproof. Butcher block gets black with a lot of water on it. Formica or a similar product and Corian do well around the sink.

3. Chopping on the counter is very handy indeed. You do not need to get chopping boards out. However there are very few counter tops that can withstand that kind of abuse. Corian is excellent. It does not injure knives, cleans easily and can be sanded when it gets rough. Butcher block will get very used looking very quickly. It is difficult to keep really clean when you chop on it. In a commercial kitchen the Board of Health frowns on it to the extent that they will not permit it in some states. It certainly does look beautiful though. A combination of butcher block and Corian or butcher block and Formica or its like quite often do well in a kitchen. Analyze the kind of cooling that you do and then pick what is best for you.

Clean Up Center

The following is a list of what might be included in the clean up center depending upon the number of people you cook for and the type of cooking and entertaining you might do.

Questions

★ What type or types of sinks do I like?

★ What type of faucets and knobs are easiest for me to handle?
★ Will instant hot water be of benefit to me?
★ Will a garbage disposal help me?
★ Will a trash compactor help me?
★ Do I wash my dishes by hand?
★ Do I wash mainly with a dish washer?
★ Where is the best place to store clean dish towels and dish towels in use?
★ Where can I put all the soaps and scrubbers?
★ Would I like a few luxuries such as a greenhouse window over the sink?

Type of Sink

Questions

★ Will I be washing by hand?
★ Will I be mainly washing with a dishwasher?
★ Do I have large pans to wash?
★ Will I be preparing a large number of fresh vegetables?
★ What surface should the sink have?
★ Do I need a drain board attached to the sink or not?

Discussion of Questions

1. If you are washing by hand most of the time then it is important to have two sinks. One sink for washing and the other for rinsing. If you have only one sink and use a plastic dishpan to rinse the dishes in, the weight of the dishpan full of water is really too much for fragile hands to lift.

2. If you will be mainly using a dishwasher you can get by with one sink. However one sink is never as efficient as two.

3. Large roasting pans are a big pain to

clean in most sinks. There are sinks that are extra large and will hold a roasting pan flat but they also take a lot of hot water to fill. How often do you use that roasting pan? If not often then forget the extra large sinks. Maybe the laundry tub would suffice if you have one for the few times you need a large sink.

4. If you do a lot of peeling of vegetables and prefer to have a garbage disposal then you might want to consider a separate sink, very small, that houses the disposal. If you have one main sink and a small one to the side this will save you from emptying the big sink every time you want to use the disposal. The Cadillac of them all is a three partition sink, a small sink in the middle with the disposal and wash and rinse sinks on either side.

5. Sinks basically come in two surfaces — porcelain enamel and stainless steel. The former comes in all sorts of decorator colors. It will not take abuse such as hockey skates clunked down on the surface while rinsing them off. Stainless steel does not stain and takes a lot of abuse. However not all sinks are the same weight so do not be fooled by pictures. Compare the different weight sinks and get what is best for you.

6. Some sinks come with a drainboard attached. They have very definite advantages such as no leaks around the sink and no wet counters but they are definitely in the luxury class so be prepared to pay handsomely for it.

Types of Faucets and Knobs

Questions

★ Do I use tall pots?
★ How fine is my grasp?
★ How strong is my grasp?

Discussion of Questions

1. Some faucets come out of the edge of the sink at a slight angle and it is impossible to put a tall pot under them. Consequently to wash a pot is a tough job. Other faucets have a gooseneck shape and almost any pot can be put under it. See page 339.

2. Knobs which take a firm grasp can be difficult to turn. See page 340. They also cause you to put pressure on your hand in a position that is not good. Levers such as the ones used in hospitals are very easy to turn on and off as they can be pushed and pulled without having to grasp them.

3. If your grasp is weak the lever type knob will probably be easiest for you to use. It is not as common as other fixtures but more and more bath and kitchen supply houses are stocking it.

Instant Hot Water

There is a very useful gadget that can be part of the battery of options such as sprays and soap dispensers. The instant hot water, see page 334, dispenses water hot enough to make instant coffee, soups and Jello. It saves you from heating water on a stove and is economical.

Garbage Disposals

Questions

★ How much food garbage do I normally have?
★ Do I peel a lot of vegetables?
★ Am I permitted to use a disposal where I live?
★ What are my other options for handling garbage?

Discussion of Questions

1. If you are cooking for a family or entertain a lot you can generate quite a bit of garbage. The disposal can save you added trips to the garbage cans. If you live in an area where it is cold and icy there is a distinct advantage to a disposal.

2. Potato peels, carrot peels and other vegetable refuse from preparing fresh vegetables can add up quickly. If you live in an area where you have a compost heap then that is a perfect place for the peelings during good weather but if not then a disposal would be of help.

3. In some areas where your home is connected to a septic tank and leach fields some feel that a disposal is not good for the system.

Trash Compactor

Questions

★ What can be put in them?
★ How much space do they take up?
★ How useful are they?

Discussion of Questions

1. Just about any trash, cans, bottles and garbage can be put into them provided it will fit inside the compactor. The compactor works with a crushing action and so what gets put into the compactor must fit inside in order to get crushed.

2. They take up considerably less space than a dishwasher or most garbage cans.

3. They are very useful for those with families where obviously more garbage is generated than if you live alone. However when the compactor bags are filled they can be VERY heavy certainly too heavy for anyone with fragile hands to lift. If you have someone that can empty the compactor for you then that would work well.

Washing Dishes by Hand

Questions

★ How many sinks do I have?
★ Is there room to let the dishes air dry in a rack?
★ Can I sit while doing the dishes?

Discussion of Questions

1. As previously mentioned under sinks two sinks are needed to do the job conveniently and get the soap off.

2. Counter space is needed in a permanent manner for air drying dishes. Continually putting away the dishrack is extra and unnecessary work. An area can be made where the dish drying racks and storage are one and the same. This can be particularly helpful if you live by yourself and do not require a big area for store/drying.

3. If standing is a problem the sink area can be designed so that you can sit on a stool and put your feet under the sink. For extended sessions at the sink this would cut down on the fatigue factor.

Washing Dishes with the Aid of a Dishwasher

Questions

★ Where should I place the dishwasher?
★ Dishwasher in general?

Discussion of Questions

1. Dishwashers are normally placed to one side or other of the sink. The side in

which it is placed usually depends upon whether you are more comfortable loading the dishwasher with your right or left hand.

2. I will not discuss brand names of dishwashers but try to give you a few pointers on what to look for when purchasing a dishwasher. Dishwashers run the gamut from a button or two to many options. If expense is a factor look at the top of the middle of the line — that usually has all the extras that are really needed. Also if you are a wine lover check to be sure the top rack will indeed handle wine glasses in an upright position. When glasses are on their side they water spot and it is very difficult to remove the spot.

Area to Store the Dish Towels
Both Clean and in Use

Questions

★ Where is the most convenient place to put a dish towel rod?
★ Where is the most convenient place to store clean dish towels?
★ Where is the best spot for paper towels?

Discussion of Questions

1. Normal places for the rod are usually under the sink. If you can place it near a radiator they will of course dry more quickly. Sometimes there is a place above the sink but that can add to the cluttered look. When all else fails there is always the handle of the drawer. Paper towels should be out and easily accessible. You also should be able to get the amount of toweling that you want, not have it whip off in sections of ten when you only want one section.

Storage of Soaps, Scrubbers and Detergents

Questions

★ How much room do I need for storage?
★ How bothersome to me is it to bend down and get things from under the sink?
★ Is their room to put my feet under the sink while sitting?
★ Are there any built-in dispensers for soap?

Discussion of Questions

1. What usually gets stored under the sink resembles, at times, a Fibber McGee's closet. Cleaning supplies are best kept not under the sink. If that is done then the soap supplies can easily be reached particularly if they are on a sliding shelf or a sliding shallow drawer.

2. If it is very difficult to bend over then the most used soaps should be kept out in something attractive. There are panels in front of the sink that can be made into a tipped drawer, see page 337, for storing steel wool and other scrubbing materials.

3. If you have a double sink for hand washing dishes then clear the area under the wash side of the sinks so that there is comfortable space for your feet. For easier access to the area the door could be removed.

4. There are all kinds of built-in dispensers that can be added to the back of the sink —including hand lotion and liquid soap dispensers which allow you to use the flat of your hand for dispensing. This action is much kinder to your hands than pinching a plastic bottle.

Also there are portable attractive liquid

soap dispenser bottles that can be filled with liquid detergent where the flat of the hand can be used.

Luxury Windows

Window greenhouses in front of the sink.

There are window units that can be put into an already existing opening or the opening can be made larger. In cold weather areas these can be a delightful addition. Herbs can be grown there all through the winter. Fresh herbs in January are very special indeed. Many window companies make these units.

Bake, Food Prep and Mix Center

Bake, Food Prep and Mix are being put together. However if you are a baker mainly, you may wish to adapt the major portion of this area to baking and vice versa. If you are not primarily a baker, you may wish to adapt the area mostly to food preparation.

In a commercial kitchen, preparation is relegated to definite areas. For instance salad preparation is not mixed in with the dessert chef. This one area "Food Prep" is probably the most import area in the kitchen. This is where you can do yourself in with fatigue if heights of counters are not correct and the design of the kitchen does not fit you.

Remember the kitchen is a place for YOU to cook not the kitchen designer, architect or non-cooking spouse. You make the decisions. Take your time in finding out what is right for you.

Some Goals in Kitchen Design Are:

★ Having a kitchen that is comfortable to work in.
★ Cutting down on fatigue by less motion and less steps and at times less standing.
★ A kitchen does not have to have everything behind closed cabinets in order to be acceptable. There are many ways in which to have everything out and accessible and still have an attractive kitchen.

Questions

★ How much baking do I do?
★ What kind of baking do I like best to do?
★ Where is it best to store small electrical appliances?
★ What kind of storage is easiest for bowls?
★ Would I like to be able to sit while performing some of the tasks?

The following is a list of what might be included in this area depending upon the kind of cooking you do and what is comfortable for you.

★ Counters at proper working height
★ Extra deep counters which allow you to put small appliances at back
★ Pastry roll out
★ Flip up counter space to add extra room
★ Swingout mixer storage in lower cabinet
★ Garage for food processor
★ Cookbook stand
★ Knife storage
★ Spice cabinet
★ Cup hooks, grid or pegboard for small utensil storage
★ Storage for baking tins
★ Handy place to get at flour
★ Designated place for sugar, honey, baking powder, etc.

357

* Shelf for mixing bowls
* Shelf space for canned items and dry items

Counters

Measure 3" below bent elbow while standing in the shoes you would normally wear for the following activities:
* Serving food
* Stacking or scraping dishes
* Making sandwiches
* Spreading mixtures on canapes
* Packaging food for storing or freezing

Measure 6" below bent elbow while standing in the shoes you would normally wear for the following activities:
* Mix batter by hand
* Knead bread
* Beat with portable mixer
* Stirring with any long handled wooden spoon or whisk

Measure 5"-7" below bent elbow while standing in the shoes you would normally wear for the following activities:
* Chopping
* Dicing
* Slicing

Extra Deep Counters

* It is important to slide as many things as possible as opposed to lifting. Anytime you must lift a heavy object out of the cabinet you are causing unnecessary fatigue and stress on your small joints.
* If your counter is extra deep that will allow you plenty of working space on the counter even though your small appliances are out on the counter

Pastry Roll Out

See page 334 for a perfect albeit expensive solution to that problem.
* Other means of handling this are to have a heavy duty pull out board or a flip up board that can be flat against the wall when not in use.

Flip Up Counter

* This can be used as an extension of a counter to give you extra room when needed but can easily be put away when not needed.

Swing Out Mixer Storage

* These units swing out then up to the proper working height. The mixer is attached to the top so that it will not go sailing off when moved.
* Try the unit before you buy it — some units move harder than others.

Garage for Food Processor

See page 321 for example.

* These keep small appliances out of sight.
* They also keep appliances less greasy.
* Try the door before you buy it to be sure you can open it with ease.

Cookbook Stand

* There are built-in ones and portable ones.
* These help your hands by keeping the books open.

★ They also keep the book cleaner.

Knife Storage

★ Have it very handy to this area.
★ See page 289-290 for the kinds of storage available.
★ Magnetic knife holders can be difficult for fragile hands. If you do not have a good grasp it is easy to knock other knives down while you are attempting to put up the ones in your hand.

Spice Cabinet

★ The food prep area is where most of the seasoning is done.
★ Steps can be saved if the storage of spices is adjacent to this area.

Storage Boards

★ Any time you do not have to rummage in a drawer for your small utensils you are protecting your joints.
★ There are many imaginative grids and boards out that can be seen at gourmet shops.

Storage for Baking Tins

★ Be sure there are dividers so that several pans do not have to be moved to get at one pan.

Handy Place for Flour

★ Remember try not to lift.
★ Have flour containers in a place where it can be slid.
★ The wonderful antique baking centers where you pull out the bin from an upper cabinet and sift out whatever you need is a gem.

Designated Place for Sugar, Honey, Baking Powder, Etc.

★ Be able to slide heavy containers.
★ Have smaller containers if possible on shallow shelves where you do not need to move jars to get at what is needed.

Shelf for Mixing Bowls

★ Put them in a sliding drawer where they do not need to be stacked more than two high.
★ A pull-out shelf or bread board with holes cut out of the board so that bowls can sit in the board and not move are a great advantage.

Shelf Space for Canned Items and Dry Items

★ See pages 315 and 333 for examples.
★ Pantry storage should be located near the food prep area with counter space nearby for unloading groceries after you have shopped.

Guidelines for Small Electrical Appliances in the Food Prep Area

Food Processors

There are many processors on the market and they come in a variety of sizes and prices. The important thing is not how it looks but how it works for you. If one model is difficult for you to handle then you will probably seldom use it and then you have not only wasted space in your kitchen but money. This is one of the few kitchen items that I do not recommend purchasing through the mail. Go to a dealer and ask if you can put the food processor together and take it apart as if to clean it. Please do NOT try many processors on the same day if your hands are very fragile — your hands will get tired and you will not be able to judge correctly what works for you. Most of the larger companies have classes at gourmet shops where you can learn how to use your processor. These classes are free — so take advantage of them and learn how to get the most from your processor.

If you and your processor are on friendly terms you will sail through most preparation with ease.

Look for the following when determining which food processor is best for you.

- ★ Ease of inserting bowl
- ★ Ease of inserting blades
- ★ Ease of locking top
- ★ Ease of engaging machine, i.e. turning a machine on and off
- ★ How difficult is it to unload?
- ★ How difficult is it to wash?
- ★ Can the base of the machine be slid?

I feel the buying of extra blades should wait until you get used to your machine and find out how you tend to use the machine. Some machines do a superb job kneading bread and they are wizards at making pie dough. They slice vegetables as thin as paper if you so desire.

I tend to use the food processor for blending and pureeing rather than the blender but you will find out in time what works best for you.

I believe firmly that a food processor is the single most important small electrical appliance in the kitchen today.

Blenders

Guidelines for Selection

- ★ How easy is it to remove the bottom for cleaning?
- ★ How difficult is it to screw the bottom on the container?
- ★ How difficult is it to set the container on the base?
- ★ How heavy is the container of the blender?
- ★ Will the blender slide?

Mixer - Stationary

Guidelines for Selection

- ★ How easy is it to remove and insert the beaters?
- ★ Does it have the speeds you need?
- ★ How many bowls does it have?
- ★ Of what are the bowls made?
- ★ Are they too heavy to lift?
- ★ Remember a full bowl is heavier than an empty one.
- ★ How easy is it to clean the beaters?
- ★ Do you have to remove the head of the mixer to insert and remove the beaters — how HEAVY is the head?
- ★ Will the mixer slide if necessary on the counter?
- ★ Will some of the attachments to the mixer be of help to me, i.e. juicer?

Mixer - Hand Held

Guidelines for Selection

- ★ How heavy is it to hold?
- ★ What tasks do I expect to have this mixer handle, i.e. take the place of a stationary mixer, light beating and mixing only. How much power does it have?
- ★ Is the length of cord adequate?
- ★ How easy is it to grasp? Will it put

stress on my hand if held for any length of time?

I do not recommend that a hand held mixer be used for heavy tasks or lengthy beating. Your hand can get very fatigued holding something of this nature for a very long time. If you enjoy baking invest in a top quality mixer. The good ones go for a long time and the companies are around if repair is needed.

Traffic Patterns

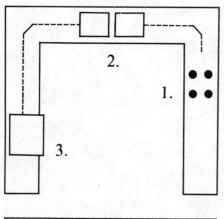

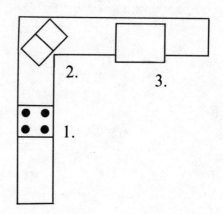

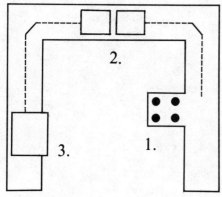

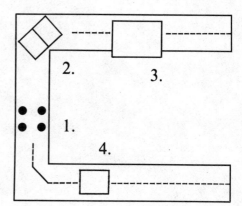

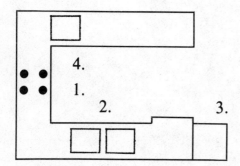

1. Stove
2. Sink
3. Refrigerator
4. Built-in Oven

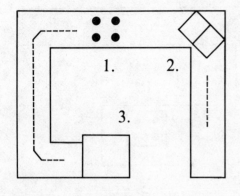

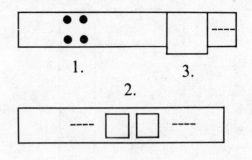

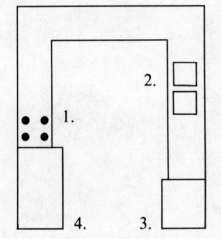

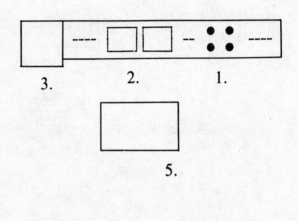

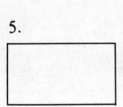

1. Stove
2. Sink
3. Refrigerator
4. Wood Stove
5. Island

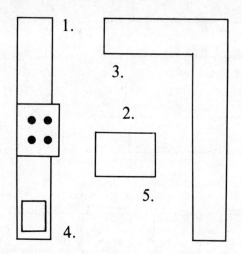

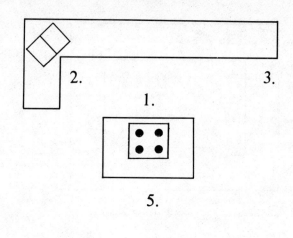

1. Stove
2. Sink
3. Refrigerator
4. Built-in Oven
5. Island

Draw your kitchen

Hints and Tips on Joint Protection

DO's

★ DO use large joints instead of small ones.

★ DO make your appliances do the work for you.

★ DO use a cart or basket that can be carried over the arm to aid in transportation of food and utensils.

★ DO be aware of how long various tasks take — so you will not do two tasks in a row that would cause undue fatigue.

★ DO use lightweight dishes and utensils.

★ DO have others help you lift and carry heavier items.

★ DO stabilize objects to lessen fatigue — such as nailboards for food and wet sponges and cloths for bowls.

★ DO sit down in a chair and stabilize bowls and cartons with knees to help stir or open carton.

★ DO have as many items as possible within easy reach.

★ DO whenever possible use the flat of the hand instead of fingers to do a task such as washing dishes.

★ DO alternate standing jobs with sitting jobs.

★ DO be sure that any task you take on is one that can be stopped part way through in case you become fatigued.

★ DO put measuring spoons in all your staples.

★ DO let guests and family help clear the table.

★ DO plan ahead.

★ DO cook several portions at one time.

★ DO when gripping or twisting your hand turn toward your thumb side.

★ DO remember that motion is good for the joints but overuse is not.

★ DO be reasonable in what you expect of yourself without babying your hands and body.

★ DO use both hands and arms whenever possible.

★ DO HAVE A POSITIVE ATTITUDE AND A SENSE OF HUMOR. BOTH WILL GET YOU THROUGH A LOT.

DON'Ts

★ DON'T force open jars with your hands — use a jar opener.

★ DON'T work at any one task for an extended time.

★ DON'T open plastic wrapped food with a knife.

★ DON'T lift heavy pots with one hand.

★ DON'T work at the incorrect work height.

★ DON'T grip handles tightly for any length of time.

★ DON'T use a manual can opener if it can be avoided.

★ DON'T use casseroles with little or no handles.

★ DON'T use a gripping twisting motion that turns toward your little finger side.

Hints and Tips

APPLES
1 pound whole = 2¾ - 3 cups peeled and sliced

ARTICHOKES
Choose large green ones with tight leaves.

ASPARAGUS
Choose thin to medium diameter. Large ones tend to be woody and stringy. Allow 6-8 ounces per person.

AVOCADO
Ripen at room temperature in a brown paper bag. It should yield slightly to the touch.

BANANAS
3 medium = 2 cups mashed
Bananas freeze well for cooking. PEEL them then put them in a plastic bag sealed tightly.

BEETS
Fresh: choose small firm ones. Cut off greens about 1½ - 2 inches above beet. Do NOT peel beet before cooking or you will have bright red water and pale beets.

BROCCOLI
Choose nonwoody stems and tightly closed buds. The stems and buds do not take the same length of time to cook. I often cook two separate meals.
First meal: Cook only flowerettes or buds.
Second meal: Use the stalks. Cut them into match sticks then parboil and finish them up by stir frying. Delicious.

BROWN RICE
1 cup raw = 4 cups cooked.
Brown rice is really worth the time it takes to cook. Combining brown rice with wild rice is an excellent combination.

BRUSSEL SPROUTS
A much maligned vegetable. Its problem has been what cooks have done to it. Over the years some people evidently thought the longer you cooked them the better the sprouts would be. Not so. Choose small closed heads. It is best to cook by the steam method then finish up by stir frying in seasoned butter. DO NOT overcook. AL DENTE only please!

BUTTER
1 stick = 4 ounces = 1/4 pound = 1/2 cup
2 sticks = 8 ounces = 1/2 pound = 1 cup
1 ounce = 2 Tablespoons

CABBAGE
1 pound head = 4½ - 6 cups shredded
This measure is approximate due to two variables — one how thick the cabbage is sliced and two whether the shredded cabbage is packed into the measure.

CANAPE ROUNDS
Wet a paper towel and spread it out on a plate. Cover it with a dry paper towel. Put the canapes on the dry paper towel and cover with foil or plastic wrap. This will keep the bread from drying out.

CANAPE RECTANGLES
Slice unsliced bread lengthwise 4-6

times depending upon the height of the bread. Then spread a canape mixture on each layer in one fell swoop so to speak. Cut the length of the bread into individual rectangular canapes.

CARROTS

1 pound = approximately 3 cups shredded

1 pound sliced serves 5-6 persons

3 ounces raw = one serving cooked

CAULIFLOWER

Choose heads that are snow white with no brown spots. The head should have tight buds.

CELERY

One average rib = 1½ - 2 ounces

Two sliced ribs = approximately 3/4 - 1 cup

CHERRY TOMATOES

1 pint = 22-26 tomatoes

CHEESE

Cheddar

1 pound = 4 - 4½ cups grated

Swiss

1/4 pound = 1 cup grated

Cheese tray

3 ounces per person

Cooking

Cheese should be cooked at a low temperature.

CHICKEN

5 pound chicken = 4½ cups cooked and diced chicken

CHERRIES

1 quart = 2 cups pitted

CRACKERS

Bremmer wafers - 54 wafers to a 4 ounce box

Carrs bite sized table wafers - 40 wafers per box

Graham crackers - 14 squares = 1 cup fine ground crumbs

Saltines - 28 crackers = 1 cup finely crushed crumbs

CREAM CHEESE

A very helpful base not only for canape spreads but also for straightening out a problem sauce.

One time when I was making a tomato based sauce at a friend's, I was in a hurry and grabbed the sweet vermouth without checking to see if it had turned or not I poured it in the sauce. I tasted the sauce and it was not only strange but not good. After adding a little of this and a little of that I put a nice big hunk of cream cheese in and that saved the day — as her guests said it was the best sauce they had ever had, would I please give them the recipe. Then what do you say, start with a bad bottle of sweet vermouth ...

CRANBERRIES

1 pound = 4 cups grated

CREAM

Half and Half is really more like a rich milk than a member of the cream family. Light Coffee Cream is indeed a member of the cream family. Will not whip. Use as an enricher.

Whipping Cream

1 cup (1/2 pint) = 2 cups whipped

Use in desserts, quiches and as garnish

CUTTING COLD OR SEMI-FROZEN FOOD

This will bring the pain very quickly so try to avoid it. If you cannot do so — then heat a knife under hot but not boiling water or you will damage the knife, and cut through whatever the food is.

DIPS

Make a day ahead for fuller flavor.

DISCOLORATION PREVENTION

Make a solution of lemon and water. Dip apples into this and it will prevent them from turning brown. However do not make the solution too strong or you will think you are eating a lemon not an apple.

EGGS

5 eggs = approximately 1 cup
8-10 egg whites = 1 cup
12-14 egg yolks = 1 cup

When cracking eggs for a recipe do not break them over the bowl in which all the ingredients have been measured. Break them into a cup then pour them into a mixing bowl. This will save you from trying to fish out any broken shells that might drip in or a bad egg.

To beat egg whites have the eggs at room temperature.

Hard cooked eggs do not peel well if the eggs are really fresh. The older eggs peel much more easily.

To cook a hard cooked egg — put egg in water, bring to boil then turn down heat to a simmer and cook 12 minutes. Remove from heat immediately drain then run under cold water.

EGGPLANT

Choose ones that are firm with no blemishes. Always salt eggplant and let it weep in a colander to drain before cooking.

FLOUR

1 pound = 3½ cups
1 pound = 5 ounces
1 pound = 4 cups sifted
1 pound cake flour = 4¾ - 5 cups sifted

FRUIT

Should be poached not stewed. They should be Al Dente not like oatmeal.

FRUIT CUT UP

One serving = 5 - 6 ounces

GARLIC

1 medium clove of garlic
1/8 teaspoon garlic powder

GARNISHES for beef and seafood

Peach halves filled with cranberry and chutney
Lemon cups filled with tartar sauce or dill sauce

GELATIN

Allow gelatin to set until it is like an unbeaten egg white — then add any ingredients that should be put in your "gelled salad."

GELATIN unflavored

1 envelope = one Tablespoon
1 Tablespoon will gel or set 2 cups of liquid

GELATIN UNMOLDING

If you have not lightly oiled the mold you will the next time.

First run a sharp knife around the edge of the mold loosening it from the sides. Wet the plate that the mold is going on slightly with cold water so that the mold will slide where you want it on the plate. Put the plate on the open side of the mold and turn over. If your hands are too fragile you will not be able to hold on to both the mold and the plate meanwhile giving it a sharp downward motion. Your method will be instead to put the plate with the mold on top of it on the counter. Wet a dish towel with hot water and squeeze as gently as you can so as not to hurt your hands. Lay the hot towel over the mold. Repeat then tap with the flat of hand. Do NOT put too many hot towels on top or you will melt the top of your gorgeous creation. Let it sit for a bit and then with a few more taps it should fall out. Good luck!

GRAPES

Tokay Grapes
1 pound = 2¾ cups seeded grapes

GRAPEFRUIT

1 medium grapefruit = 2/3 cup juice
1/2 grapefruit has approximately 12 sections

GRAVY

Freeze left over gravy in an ice cube tray. When frozen transfer the cubes to a plastic bag that can be sealed. To use — remove the number of cubes needed and heat slowly.

GREEN BEANS

Choose small slender crisp ones
One serving = 4 ounces per person
One pound fresh beans = 4 servings

GREEN PEPPER

1 large pepper = 1 cup diced

GREENS (Lettuce)

Bibb Lettuce: Small heads require a great deal of rinsing as soil manages to get way down in it. Do NOT tear the leaves — they are usually small enough to leave whole.

Boston/Butter Lettuce: Very tender, tear the large leaves keeping the small leaves whole. The very tiny leaves at times can be bitter.

Chicory/Curley Endive: Crisp with a slightly bitter taste. I prefer it combined with other greens.

Endive — Belgian or French: Requires little cleaning, do not tear the leaves use them whole. It has a very slight bitter taste but very refreshing. Leaves may also be stuffed for appetizers.

Iceberg/Head Lettuce: It is not a favorite of mine. I do however, mix it with other greens when making large salads. In food value it receives just about a zero.

Leaf Lettuce: A wonderful lettuce as it comes straight from your garden with a delicate dressing on a hot summer day. However it droops quickly so do not keep a lot on hand. Let it sit in your garden until you need it. I wash then spin dry and store in slightly damp paper towels.

Romaine: A head type lettuce with long leaves. Does not droop easily thus is good for a caesar salad that requires a lot of tossing. Do not use the very coarse outer leaves — save those for soup. Tear leaves in big pieces. This lovely lettuce has a great deal of food value.

Watercress: You either love it or hate it. Choose bunches with no yellow. It wilts quickly. A delight as a garnish instead of parsley. Watercress and parsley keep well in an air tight jar in the refrigerator. Wash, drain and dry well before storing.

LEMONS

Juice of 1 lemon = 2-3 Tablespoons
Roll lemon with flat of hand and it will yield more juice. Put lemon in hot water for a few minutes and it will also yield more juice. Usually the thinner the skin the more the juice.

LIMES

Juice of 1 lime = 1½-1 Tablespoons
To yield more juice see lemons.

MELONS

The very tasty melons show off their bouquet and aroma best when not served too cold. Cool yes, but not ice cold.

Cantaloupe: Choose one good in color and which the ends give when pushed. Yield, approximately 12 ounces cut up fruit per melon.

Casaba: Flesh is white. When it is ripe it is very, very good and when not ripe it is tasteless.

Crenshaw: Flesh is orange, a real prince of a melon.

Honeydew: Flesh is green. I shake

them and if the seeds rattle they are ripe but I am not sure the green grocer will like to have his or her melons shaken a dozen times a day.

Persian: Flesh is orange, larger than cantaloupe, absolutely delicious when ripe.

Watermelon: Flesh is pink to red. It can be very sweet — an American summer tradition eating watermelon.

MUSHROOMS

Choose ones with tight caps and light in color for salads. Over the hill mushrooms can be diced in a food processor for soups or stuffings.

1 pound = 20-24 medium mushrooms
1 pound fresh = 8 ounce can sliced
Save liquid from canned mushrooms and use in soups

NUTS

Almonds
1 pound = 3 cups chopped
Pecan Halves
1 pound = 4½-5 cups
Walnuts
1 pound = 4 cups chopped

ONION

1 medium = 1/2 cup chopped
1 medium = 2½ - 3 ounces
1 pound sliced or diced = 3½ - 4 cups
White onions tend to be milder than yellow. Frozen chopped onions behave better when they have been patted dry on a paper towel before being used.

ONION PEELING

Let's deal with this unfavorite task of most cooks. There must be over a hundred ways to handle onions without tears. Believe me in the food business I have heard of many. Let me list a few.

1. Put a piece of bread in your mouth then tackle the onion.

2. Peel the whole onion except near the top or is it the foot. Supposedly only when the ends are cut do you have trouble.

3. Put the onion in the freezer for 5 minutes, no more no less "they" say.

4. Run water in sink before you peel. Put onion under running water while you peel.

5. Hold a cut potato in your mouth while peeling.

6. My best method was somewhat amusing. I was and maybe still am a scuba diver. I put my mask and snorkel on and then tackled the onion. Now that did work but it certainly did freak out customers and delivery people.

ORANGES

Juice of one average orange = 1/3-1/2 cup

PAPRIKA

A spice that indeed has taste. The finest is Hungarian. It comes in a mild flavor up to strong. Store in the refrigerator in a tin or ceramic container — do not expose to light.

PEARS AND PEACHES

4 medium = 2 cups sliced

PEAS

Fresh 1 pound whole = 1 cup shelled
Frozen 10 ounce package = 1½ cups cooked

POTATO, SWEET

3 medium = 3 cups sliced

POTATO, WHITE

3 medium = 2 cups cubed and cooked
1 pound unpeeled = 2 cups mashed or 4 servings
3 medium sized baking potatoes = approximately 1 pound

1. Avoid those with green patches or tiny cuts.

2. Choose potatoes that are approximately the same size as they will cook in the same length of time.

3. Store in a cool dark place.

4. Do not store and use from the refrigerator. They will turn gray when cooked.

5. A little lemon juice added to the potatoes just before you drain off the water will make whiter mashed potatoes.

6. Do not store them next to the refrigerator, dishwasher, stove or ovens. Those storage areas are not cool.

RASPBERRIES
1/2 pound (8 ounces) = 1⅓ cups whole
1/2 pound = a little less than 1 cup seived

RICE
1 cup raw = 3 cups cooked

SHELLFISH
CRAB
Alaskan King — legs often split and broiled

Dungeness — legs quite meaty with a good taste, very versatile to cook with

Florida Back Fin — used for salads, sold in cans

Stone Crab Claws — served cracked but whole with melted butter

4-5 ounces crabmeat per serving

Soft-shelled crabs (Blue crabs without their shells) usually 2-3 per person

SHRIMP
Usually sold by the count per pound
40 per pound = small
26-30 = medium or large depending upon location
20-26 = large depending upon location
16-20 = large depending upon location
10-16 = usually considered jumbo

To cook: Put shrimp in cold water, bring to boil, drain immediately and run under cold water to stop cooking process.

Fresh celery leaves added to water while cooking shrimp does cut down on the odor.

Fresh frozen shrimp should be ivory colored not white. If white they are probably freezer burned.

SPAGHETTI
1 ounce package = 3-4 cups cooked

SPINACH CHOPPED
10 ounce frozen package = 1/2 cup with moisture squeezed out

STRAWBERRIES
1 quart = 4 cups sliced
1 quart = 2 cups pureed

SUGAR
1 pound brown = approximately 2½ cups packed
1 pound granulated = 2½ cups
1 pound confectioners unsifted = 4½ cups

TOMATOES
Fresh 1 pound whole = 1/2 cups peeled seeded and without juice
1 (35 ounce) can Italian tomatoes = 1¾ cups strained

Herbs   Spices   Seasonings

Herb	Used With
ALLSPICE	Whole in pickling, ground in pot roasts
BASIL	Tomatoes, eggplant, beans, salad and salad dressing, poultry, fish, stews, Italian dishes, in bouquet garni
BAY LEAVES	Tomato dishes, stews, soups, stocks and marinades
CAPERS	Fish, chicken, salads and garnishes
CELERY SEEDS	Salads and salad dressing, stews, stocks and soups
CHERVIL	Salads and salad dressing, fine herbs, stuffed eggs, egg dishes, spinach, seasoned butter, veal, poultry
CHILI POWDER	Is made from several ingredients — chili peppers, cumin, oregano, garlic and salt
CHIVES	Salads, eggs, cheese (cottage and cream) dips, soups, poultry
CUMIN	Mexican dishes, an ingredient in curry, soups and some tomato dishes
CURRY POWDER	A blend of spices — usually including tumeric, ginger and cumin
DILL WEED	Scandinavian dishes, fish, potatoes, string beans, salads and salad dressings, soups
GARLIC	Presently it seems to go into almost everything
JUNIPER BERRY	Game, poultry and gin
MACE	Part of the nutmet, cakes, stews, preserving
MARJORAM	Cheeses, mushrooms, fish, veal, meatloaf, stuffings and salads
NUTMEG	Stews, sauces, soups, quiches and custards
MSG	Increases flavor, Chinese dishes
OREGANO	Tomatoes, string beans, salads and salad dressing, marinades, poultry, veal, pot roasts, stews, eggs
PARSLEY	Mushrooms, soups, stocks, stews, salads, vegetables and garshing
PIMENTO	From the sweet pepper — salads, garnishing for cold vegetables such as asparagus
POULTRY SEASONING	Usually a combination of sage, marjoram, thyme, savory, celery seed, minced onion and pepper
ROSEMARY	Tomatoes, fish, lamb, pork, meatloaf, stuffings, egg and cheese dishes, bouquet garni

SAGE	Stuffings, poultry, veal, tomatoes, cheeses
SAVORY	Fish, poultry stuffings, meat sauces, beans, egg dishes and bouquet garni
SHALLOTS	Use as you would garlic
TARRAGON	Poultry, fish, egg dishes, salads and salad dressings, sauces, mushrooms, tomatoes
THYME	Stews, soups, stocks, stuffings, veal, poultry, Creole dishes, bouquet garni
TUMERIC	In curry powder, meat and egg dishes
BOUQUET GARNI	1. Equal parts basil, thyme, marjoram and savory
	2. Bay leaf, parsley, thyme and celery
FINE HERBS	Chervil, chives, parsley and tarragon
HERBS OF PROVENCE	Equal parts thyme, basil, summer savory and fennel

Hints and Tips on Ways to Help for Spouses, Friends and Family

Grating a few pounds of cheese — then bagging it in amounts you would normally use in cooking. For instance two pounds of grated cheese bagged in 1/2 cup amounts.

Grating premade roux

Chopping or grating nuts

Making and packaging bread crumbs

Removing frozen cubes of gravy or stock from trays and packaging them

Cutting chicken breasts in finger length strips. Then package and freeze chicken in serving amounts (2, 4, 6)

Filling liquid soap containers from larger one. Small containers are easier for fragile hands to operate.

Emptying staples into slidable canisters.

Filling decanters for cooking with sherry, madeira or brandy. The decanters themselves stay out on the counter and are easy to open.

Open olive jars and the like that can be stored in the refrigerator after opened

Make ahead herb combinations of provence, bouquet garni, or fine herbs

Sharpening knives

Shopping from the cook's list

Carrying in the groceries

Getting out of reach items within reach before you leave

Directory

Directory

Hints and Tips on Shopping by Mail

Shopping by mail can save you endless fatigue, stress and frustration. Being able to do it at your leisure is a great plus. You also do not have to shop when the store is open. However, remember a few things when buying in this manner.

★ You will be paying postage and handling.

★ You should comparison shop between catalogues as large items in particular can vary in price a great deal.

★ When you add up your purchases you may be surprised how much it costs you to have it sent but you have not had to pay transportation to get to a store or wait in line waiting to be served.

★ Some companies charge for their first catalogue. Cash can certainly be sent but it is safer to send a check or money order.

★ Occasionally companies will give you credit for the cost of their catalogue toward your first purchase which seems a fair way to do it.

★ Be sure the company offers you a money back guarantee.

★ If you have doubts about the reliability of the concern check with the Better Business Bureau near the company. Your local Bureau can give you their address.

★ Order from a current catalogue. If you do not have a current one write them that yours is out of date and they should send you one free.

★ There are rules governing the mail order business:

1. The company must send what you have ordered within 30 days. If they are out of stock they must let you know there is a delay and give you the option for a full refund.

2. If you develop a problem with the firm contact MAIL ACTION LINE, Direct Mail Marketing Association, 6 East 43rd Street, New York, NY 10017. Send the name of the company, state the nature of your problem and send a COPY of your cancelled check, money order or credit card slip.

3. When all else fails write the Attorney General of the state in which the company is located. However do step two before you resort to this.

I have not stated where each piece of equipment comes from nor the price as the companies change what they have in their catalogues and prices do vary from company to company.

There are many items due to space that had to be left out of the book — so as you go through the catalogues let your imagination work for you and see what you can find that might help you perform a task that has given you problems bearing in mind that you do not want to have your hand get forced in a position where it goes toward the little finger side — known as Ulnar deviation.

The following companies carry items mostly related to cooking and the kitchen.

Brookstone
5 Vose Farm Road
Peterborough, NH 03458

The Chef's Catalog
3915 Commercial Avenue
Northbrook, IL 60062

Colonial Garden Kitchens
270 West Merrick Road
Valley Stream, LI 11582

Cook's Corner
P.O. Box 2727
Del Mar, CA 92014

Copco
2240 West 75th Street
Woodridge, IL 60517

The Corning Source
P.O. Box 2033
Nashua, NH 03061-2033

The Crate and Barrel
195 Northfield Road
Northfield, IL 60093

Especially for Cooks
Sears, Roebuck and Co.
Sears Tower
Chicago, IL 60684

Europa Design
50 Cole Parkway
Scituate Harbor, MA 02066

Figi's Collection for Cooking
Marshfield, WI 54404

Garlic Press
450 Sutter Street
P.O. Box 77904
San Francisco, CA 94607

Kitchen Bazaar
4455 Connecticut Avenue, N.W.
Washington, DC 20008

Kitchen Glamor
26770 Grand River
Redford, MI 48240

Le Gourmand
(Butcherblock Furniture)
Taylor Woodcraft
P.O. Box 245
Malta, OH 43758-0245

Maid of Scandinavia
#244 Raleigh Avenue
Minneapolis, MN 55416

Williams — Sonoma
Mail Order Department
P.O. Box 7456
San Francisco, CA 94120-7456

The Wooden Spoon
Route 5, P.O. Box 852
Mahopac, NY 10541

World's Fair
P.O. Box 5678
Smithtown, NY 11787

The following companies have a great deal of items related to cooking and the kitchen.

Dansk
Dansk International Designs Ltd.
Mount Kisco, NY 10549

Gazin's
P.O. Box 19221
New Orleans, LA 70179

Hammacher Sclemmer
South East Operations Center
115 Brand Road
Salem, VA 24156

Holst, Inc.
1118 West Lake, Box 370
Tawas City, MI 48763

Joan Cook
P.O. Box 21628
Ft. Lauderdale, FL 33335

Lilian Vernon
510 South Fulton Ave.
Mount Vernon, NY 10550

Specialties of the House
3601 N.W. 15th Street
Lincoln, NE 68544

Taylor Gifts
P.O. Box 206
Wayne, PA 19087

The following companies have some items related to cooking and the kitchen.

Adam York
Unique Merchandise Mart
Bldg. 6
Hanover, PA 17333

Ambassador
711 West Broadway
Tempe, AZ 85266

American Treasury
P.O. Box 1343
Largo, FL 34294

Artisan Galleries
4120 Main Street
Dallas, TX 75226

Bloomingdale's by Mail
115 Brand Road
Salem, VA 24156

Boston Proper Mail Order
P.O. Box 2027
Nashua, NH 03061

Bruce Bolind
484 Bolind Bldg.
P.O. Box 9751
Boulder, CO 80301

Camping World
P.O. Box C.W.
Bowling Green, KY 42102-4920

Carefree House
711 W. Broadway
Tempe, AZ 85282

Collwell Collection
201 Kenyon Road
Champaign, IL 61820

Comfortably Yours
(Aids for easier living)
52 West Hunter Avenue
Maywood, NJ 07607

Community Kitchens
P.O. Box 3778
Baton Rouge, LA 70821-3778

Conran's
145 Hugenot Street
New Rochelle, NY 10801

Country Loft
(Wood Accessories)
South Shore Park
Hingham, MA 02043

Country Notebook
Renovator's Old Mill
Millers Falls, MA 01349

Clymer's of Bucks County
141 Canal Street
Nashua, NH 03061-2007

Delectable Country Things
Northshore Farmhouse
Greenhurst, NY 14742

Eddie Bauer
P.O. Box 3700
Seattle, WA 98124

Fashion Able Self-Help Items
Box S
Rocky Hill, NJ 08553

Features
2575 Chantily Drive, N.E.
Atlanta, GA 30324-9990

Gallery of Amsterdam
Wallin's Corner Road
Amsterdam, NY 12010-1893

Giggletree
Winterbrook Way
Meredith, NH 03253

Hanover House
Unique Merchandise Mart
Bldg. 2
Hanover, PA 17333

Harriet Carter
North Wales, PA 19455

Hoffritz
515 W. 24th Street
New York, NY 10114-0041

Horchow Collection
P.O. Box 819066
Dallas, TX 75381-9066

The James Company
3200 S.E. 14th Avenue
Ft. Lauderdale, FL 33316

Jennifer House
New Marlboro Stage
Great Barrington, MA 01230

Johnny Appleseed's
50 Dodge Street
Beverly, MA 01915

Leichtung
4944 Commerce Parkway
Cleveland, OH 44128

Lynchburg Hardware & General Store
(Oven Stick)
Lynchburg, TN 37352

Markline
P.O. Box C-5
Belmont, MA 02178

Miles Kimbel
41 West 8th Avenue
Oshkosh, WI 54906

New Hampton
Unique Merchandise
Bldg. 10
Hanover, PA 17333

Old Village Shop
Unique Merchandise
Bldg. 8
Hanover, PA 17333

Orvis (Christmas Catalog)
10 River Road
Manchester, VT 05254

Paprikas Weiss Importer
1546 Second Avenue
New York, NY 10028

Paragon
P.O. Drawer 511
Westerly, RI 02891

Pennsylvania Station
Unique Merchandise Mart
Bldg. 14
Hanover, PA 17333

Pier 1 Imports
500 Forest Park Blvd.
Ft. Worth, TX 76102-5899

The Plow and Hearth
560 Main Street
Madison, VA 22727

Pot-Pour-Ri
204 Worcester
Wellesly, MA 02181

Pottery Shack
1212 So. Coast Highway
Laguana Beach, CA 92651

Rainbow of Gifts
Unique Merchandise Mart
Bldg. 30
Hanover, PA 17333

Russell's
450 Sutter Street
P.O. Box 77904
San Francisco, CA 94107

S.F. Rykoff and Co.
P.O. Box 21467
Market Street Station
Los Angeles, CA 90021

The Sharper Image
406 Jackson Street
San Francisco, CA 94111

Shelburne Company
110 Painters Mill Road
Owings Mills, MD 21117

Spencer Gifts
871 Spencer Bldg.
Atlantic City, NJ 08411

Sturbridge Village Workshop
Blueberry Road
Westbrook, ME 04092

Tapestry
Unique Merchandise Mart
Bldg. 46
Hanover, PA 17333

Triffles
P.O. Box 819075
Dallas, TX 75381-9075

Valerie Choice
Linwood Square
Linwood, NY 08221

Vermont Country Store
Weston and Rockingham
Weston, VT 05161

Yield House
Department 8950
North Conway, NH 03860

Walter Drake
Drake Bldg.
Colorado Springs, CO 80940

Woodline
(Knives)
1731 Clement Avenue
Alameda, CA 94501

Glossary of Cooking Terms

BAKE — To cook in an oven.

BASTE — To moisten food with a liquid by brushing on with a pastry brush or spooning a liquid over the food.

BLEND — To combine two ingredients or more until it is thoroughly mixed.

BOIL — Cooking in liquid that is over 212° F where the bubbles are large.

BRAISE — Step one is to brown in a small amount of fat or oil. Step two is to finish cooking by simmering until done in an inch of liquid.

BROWN — To cook over high heat in a small amount of fat sealing in the juice.

CHILL — To refrigerate until the food has become cold.

COOL — To reduce heat by pulling the pan off the burner.

DEGLAZE — To pour liquid (stock, wine or water) into a saucepan where food has been browned and pick up all those good brown nubbins.

GREASE — To spread lightly with butter or shortening.

MARINATE — Usually to submerge food in wine or vinegar with seasonings.

MELT — To heat a solid shortening or fat until it has become liquid.

POACH — To cook in stock, water or wine or a combination thereof where the bubbles are small as in simmer.

PUREE — To change the consistency of the food from solid or semi-solid to a liquid state — usually done with a food processor, blender or manually pushed through a sieve.

REDUCE — To cook liquid down to a more concentrated state over medium high heat.

ROUX — Flour and butter in equal parts cooked together — then used to thicken sauce.

SAUTÉ — To quickly cook over medium high heat in a small amount of fat.

STEAM — To cook food on a rack or in a steamer not allowing the food to come in contact with the water.

WHIP — To beat food such as cream or egg white until stiff.

About the Author

Beverly Bingham, an arthritic has written a unique book which brings to the public and to the therapist a resource book as well as a cookbook. She has drawn on her many years of knowledge as a therapist and chef, combining the two in this helpful and hopeful book, *COOKING WITH FRAGILE HANDS*.

Prior to writing *COOKING WITH FRAGILE HANDS*, Mrs. Bingham mailed over 1,000 questionnaires to Occupational Therapy Departments throughout the USA, requesting information on how best to fulfill the needs of those who cook with fragile hands. She received an overwhelming and positive response as well as many suggestions. These suggestions along with her considerable knowledge as chef and therapist are her response to an area of cooking which is not provided elsewhere.

Mrs. Bingham received her B.A. from the University of Rochester and her degree in Occupational Therapy from the University of Pennsylvania. She holds the title of Dame Maître Rôtisseur in the prestigious International food society of the Chaine des Rôtisseur.